ALL SORTS
of thoughts

POETRY AND PROSE
BY PAULINE LATTER

07719 741248
platter342@gmail.com

Copyright © Pauline Latter 2022

The rights of Pauline Latter to be identified as author of this work has been asserted by her in accordance with the Copyright, Designs and Patents Act 1988

This collection first published 2022

All Rights Reserved. No part of this publication may be reproduced or transmitted in any form or by any means, electronic or mechanical including photocopying, recording, or any information storage and retrieval system, without permission in writing from the author.

Published for Pauline Latter by Verité CM Ltd.

ISBN No: 978-1-914388-30-9

Design, typesetting, print and production management by Verité CM Ltd, Worthing, West Sussex BN12 4BG UK.

www.veritecm.com

Introduction to the Author

As a child, when I was taken to visit my grandparents, I was given a battered old attaché case with notepads and receipt books, to keep me quiet I suspect.

That was when my love of writing started – poems and short stories (which I still have!) and, succeeding in English Language at school encouraged me further.

Working, motherhood and then working again didn't leave me much time for hobbies but, with the blessing of retirement came a fresh outpouring.

The written word can have different meanings and cause different emotions to each individual depending on their upbringing, sense of humour, traumas, lifestyle, preferences and what mood they're in at the time.

I can't always understand other people's poetry so I have written simply from my heart, as I have experienced or with my vivid imagination, in a style that I prefer and hope you will too.

Sad things like the Pandemic don't feature much as I believe in trying to keep positive and joyful. I hope you have a good chuckle and don't worry too much about the state of my mind!

Index

Chilean Miners 11
Watery Journey 12
Shanklin 14
Earth's Moon 15
Greetings 16
The Handsome Stranger 17
Death by Chocolate 18
The Lonely Legionnaires 19
The Sound of Silence 20
Slipping Through the Net 21
My Train 22
Summer Heat 23
My Bit of Jigsaw 24
Paul 26
Life's Not a Box of Chocolates 27
Indian Summer 28
It's Good to be Alive 29
This Cat 30
Last Day on the Beach 31
He's Late 32
West Beach 33
Fingle's Cave 34
Seeking Peace 35
The Last Gift 36
The Old Apple Tree 37

A Sense of Place 38
The First Snowfall 39
A Late Spring Walk 40
An Acquired Taste 42
Ashes to Ashes 43
That First Day 44
The Day we went to Leonardslea 45
The Somme 46
Marked for Life 48
Something Strange 49
Ammerdown 50
Foolish, Fearless or Fun? 52
We Had to Flee 53
The Magical, Misty Moment 54
The Long, Long Wait 56
Circles of My Life 57
VE Day Celebration 58
The Hard Climb 59
The Year 2016 60
Our Daily Gift 62
Listen to Your Heart 63
Fox in the Garden 64
The Oyster Pond 65
Memories of Lake Garda 66
My Little Bit of Heaven 68
Other People's Words 69
The Unprovable 70

Our Town 71
The Blob 72
Where to Go 73
One Shop Wonder 74
May Day in Lydney Park 75
Nature's Worst 76
The Kitchen Waltz 77
Choices 78
Hot Summer 79
The White Walk 80
Little Boy Jonathan 81
On Eagles' Wings 82
Through the Old Wooden Door 84
My Russian Dolls 85
A Stroll in the Late Spring Sun 86
Going Sunbathing 88
Willpower 89
Irritations 90
Me and the Spider 91
Depreciation 92
What to Eat 93
Growing Old Disgracefully 94
The Picnic 95
The Shower Pole 96
Poppy Poo 97
Embarrassment 98
My Initial Thought 100

Junk Mail	101
Underthings	102
The Passenger	104
A Safari Story	106
Gone Fishing	107
Dangerwoman	108
The Woolly Coffins	109
How Did We Manage?	110
The Gremlin in the Oven	111
Just a Check-up	112
Groundwater Day	114
Standing in an English Queue	115
The Perfect Cake	116
Sticky Stuff	118
The Silent Hour	119
Time to Waste	120
Walkies	122
Woolacombe Beach	124
Incensed or What?	125
Don't Let the Biscuits Bully You	126
Jammy Days	127
Flight of Fancy	128
In the Grip of the Invisible Monster	129
The Age Gap Rap	130
The Sticky End	131
The Lost Stripes	132
Space Bake	133

My One Hour Dilemma	134
Shedding Ideas	135
Pandemic Prose	136
Lockdown Town	138
Speeding Along the Prom	139
The Twelve Weeks of Christmas	140
Reigning For Seventy Years	142

Chilean Miners

Down in the darkness people sat,
Weak and tired, cold and hungry.
Would they ever see light again
And faces of their friends and family?

"We're lost" they thought, "we can't be saved,
We're too far down, there is no air".
One by one they drowned in sorrow,
Hope giving way to deep despair.

But Someone knew and Someone cared
And Someone did just all He could.
He made a way to save those men,
He had a plan and it was good.

The hole was very narrow at first,
But hope was born with fresh air in that place.
Then the water and then the food
And a camera to catch the joy on a face.

Then a man descended to that hellish place,
He'd come to give them a second chance.
They saw and believed and were raised above
Where they cried and cheered and praised and danced.

Watery Journey

The sullen, forbidding, scowling clouds give up their watery contents on to the higher hills, and the thirsty earth devours it greedily. It saturates the surface soil, permeates the chalk and rock – down and down until it appears out of a crack and a gap, springing from earth to greet the air.

It trickles over the mossy rocks, and splashes the lush green ferns. It chuckles and chatters under the canopy of shadowy trees, through a tangle of brown crochet, pulling leaves and insects into its gentle flow. It winds and meanders under a rainbow of sinuous branches – a heavenly tunnel.

Suddenly it emerges into the light of open moorland, still a murmuring, babbling brook, pulled by the unseen hand of gravity.

Other tiny becks join in the swelling stream, and the bubbling chorus becomes a sonorous choir. There are sounds in the air like the little Water Babies shrieking with joyous laughter.

Gathering speed and strength, the thundering torrent surges onward, down into the gash sliced through the hills long ago – cleaving and tearing; splitting and lacerating; shifting stones; pushing pebbles; rolling rocks and breaking boulders.

Still descending; plunging; tumbling; cascading over escarpments and bluffs with so much energy like someone's turned on a hundred taps or flushed a thousand toilets – whooshing and shooshing, onwards, forwards, downwards – calling out raucously "Make way – I'm coming!"

One more hill to slice through and – the view opens wide its watery arms and fills the air with its salty tang.

A panorama of reflecting sparkle; a vision of light and space and a blaze of brilliance.

The slowing stream exhales, exhausted, sapped of its strength, widens out and ripples its way through shallow gullies across the sand, over gravel and pebbles, round sea rocks covered with bladder wrack.

Fresh water, overwhelmed by brine, mingles and merges and blends into the vast expanse of the sea at its journey's end.

Shanklin

Hot and dry, the dusty road rewards me
With a tranquil oasis called 'The Chine'.
Sitting, alone, birdsong delighting my spirit,
Dappled shade, restoring my soul.

The sound of gurgling water below me
Refreshes my innermost parts.
Peace, like a blanket, surrounds and envelopes me,
Calming, soothing, replenishing, ministering.

Down and down the fern-lined steps,
Reaching nearer and nearer the sound of surf.
Into the brilliant sunshine that startles my senses,
Waking my cooled skin to the warmth of summer.

Sitting, alone, by the sandy shore,
The never-ending waves with their white-crested breakers
Coating the mustard sands
And giving up their strands of glistening seaweed.

The tankers in the distance, slicing through the Channel,
White sails of yachts gliding along at leisure,
Children playing happily, gulls wheeling – looking for lunch.
Sights and sounds and senses, all in unison and harmony.

Earth's Moon

O big blowzy Moon in a pitch-black void
Shining your silvery light for all mankind
To enjoy, to marvel at, to absorb
All your craters and pock-marks –
Scars that tell of your journey through time.

O midnight Moon who, at Earth's passing turns blood-red
For all who care to stay awake for your rare exhibition.
From my quiet garden I wait for you to change –
Like watching a peacock unfold his eye-filled plumage,
You don't disappoint.

O Jerusalem Moon, shining over the city,
Lighting up the roof tops
And the myriad of ancient tombs below me.
That same sight that Jesus saw long ago –
Same Moon – but new dome.

O mid-day Moon, who had the power
To turn on the street lights
When you hid the Sun's face from us hordes
On Highdown Hill.

O crescent Moon, someone has taken
Such a perfect bite out of your silver side
As you lazily sail across the black velvet –
Just missing all those little sparkling diamonds
That surround you.

*(Highdown's eclipse wasn't as dark as Bodmin,
but then not so many traffic jams!)*

Greetings

What is expected of me nowadays
When I greet somebody new?
How many kisses on how many cheeks
Or will a handshake do?

Yes, a handshake's right for a business deal,
I know where I stand with that.
And I know what my friends are going to do
When we meet up for a chat.

But the folk I don't know very well
Don't know what I may do,
So the slightest lean to the left or right
Shows a kiss or hug is due.

Now is it to be a lips-on-cheek
Or a 'mwa' into thin air?
And if it's a sticky or sweaty cheek
Do I show that I don't care?

Some people from another land
May go for two or three,
And if the arms are outstretched wide
A big bear-hug's for me.

So, once we've greeted in whatever way
And we've talked til all is plain,
What do we do to say goodbye?
Go through it all again?

The Handsome Stranger

I wonder what he was thinking
As I gazed into his eyes,
And was my visit expected,
Or was I a big surprise?

I could see myself reflected
In those great big pools of brown;
Was he looking into my eyes too
Or looking me up and down?

I told him he was handsome
And he was God's creation;
Did he realise he was special –
And the pride of all his nation?

His breath was gentle near my face,
His nostrils quivered slightly.
He listened to my whispering,
His lips touched my hand so lightly.

Tomorrow, on show, he'll be prancing around
Like a stately Spanish galleon,
But just for a moment, right now, he's mine –
This proud white Lipica stallion.

(The Lipizzaner horses at the Lipica Stud Farm, Slovenia)

Death By Chocolate

Got a sweet tooth but boiled sweets and toffees just won't do.
Is it the fat? But cheap choc is 'bleeere'.
Gotta be good choc – dark or milk.
Look at that colour – shape doesn't matter.
Smell that aroma – reminds me of childhood Easter eggs.
Smell again before tasting – fill up my senses – starting to dribble!
Lick the smoothness – nibble the edges – taste buds exploding!
Get it round my tongue – over the roof – around the palette.
Oh delicious – oh joy – oh satisfying.
But is it? As it slides, melting, liquefying, down my throat
I want another – and another – and another.
Can't stop at one or two – am I addicted?
Am I hiding it away so I can delve in when the cravings start?
Am I always thinking of it?
Have I written a poem about it?!
Does it affect my life – my sleep – my finances?
What's the fat doing to my arteries – will it fur me up?
I've told my loved ones I want an eco coffin in the design of a box of chocs.
Is there a song about chocolate that could be played at my demise?

But hey – they say it's good for you – so I'm all right then.
Pass me another chocolate please.

The Lonely Legionnaires

So far from home and achingly cold,
They served their years in the Great Wall's fort
Keeping the wild barbarians out.
Frost-bitten toes; and diseases they caught.

High on the gatehouse, eyes peeled for the foe,
Or polishing swords to keep them from damp;
Those Legionnaires loyal to beloveds in Rome,
Or lonely and tempted by "ladies" near the camp.

Some lasted their years and received their small pension,
Went home to their wives who may have remained loyal.
Some stayed with their local girl and fathered a child,
But many remained as white bones in the soil.

The Sound of Silence

(sitting by the shore of Llyn Gwynant with Snowden in the background)

Sitting on the pebbly beach
Watching the ripples endlessly flow.
A gurgling stream nearby competes.
Where will all this moving water go?

Across the lake the mountains rise –
Lofty crags of green and grey.
Shadows of clouds are racing across,
Chasing the bird that swoops on prey.

The cuckoo calls in the lakeside trees,
A lone sheep bleats as it climbs up to the skies.
On every side a twittering sound
And dark shapes flash as they catch the flies.

The silence broken by a passing car
That jars against nature's sweetest sounds,
But I focus again on the scene ahead –
A sight for sore eyes that knows no bounds.

Slipping Through the Net

In this civilised country of ours
With its Welfare and Benefits net,
How come there are folk who are hungry,
Who can't remember the last time they ate?

In this land of Lottery millions
Where its bankers' huge bonuses get,
How come there are so many homeless
And many more going into debt?

In the places where elderly and lonely
Have only the company of a pet,
How come they're not able to replace them
'Cause they cannot afford a vet?

All round us are people who're breaking
'Cause basic needs are not being met.
How come there are so many holes
In our wonderful Welfare net?

My Train
(coming back from Wales)

Hordes of sweaty bodies – all shapes and sizes and weights,
Crushed together like sardines in a can called a train.
Only two carriages – people for six –
How to cram them in, cheek by jowl, shoulder by shoulder?

Suitcases, one upon the other until bulging into the aisle:
Overhead racks dripping with straps of haversacks, rucksacks, backpacks.
Legs in the gangway – step over – step around – step on!
Swearing, apologising, sighs, grunts, giggles.

How to eat? How to breathe? How to stretch out
Those cramped, aching legs, entwined around other feet?
Don't have to mind touching, kicking, pushing.
Bags on tables – books on bags – coats on racks – stuff on laps.

Baby crying – voicing for us all. Toddler whining – how much longer?
Need the toilet? Disrupt all around. Which direction?
Keep focussed – it *will* end. Could be worse – horse and cart?
I've got a seat – by a window – and lunch – and a book!
And air conditioning – not so bad!

Summer Heat

Winter's clinging tentacles have lost their grip at last,
The icy fingers just a sad and dismal memory.

Oh warmth, wrap me up like a blanket,
Welcome friend, you've been gone so long.

Hot, dry, long dusty days,
With warm golden evenings as the shadows lengthen.

Stuffy, sticky, sultry nights,
Tossing, turning, bedding flung asunder.

Sun burning skin, searing, scorching,
Oh shade, oh breeze, cool me!

Rumbling thunder, lightning flash,
Rain approaching, birds quiet.

Lashing, rattling, shredding shards,
Oh cool sweet air, washing, refreshing, oh bliss!

My Bit of Jigsaw

I'm shut in a box with hundreds of other pieces of jigsaw – crowded, huddled, sat upon, sitting on. In a polythene bag to keep us from wandering or getting lost.

The box is opened and childish hands pick up the bag and empty the contents on to a table. Ouch, I've fallen upside-down with one of my edges locked into another piece.

We're all turned face-up so I can see the young child above me. I'm so excited – what piece am I?

I don't know who I am yet so I wait patiently to be chosen. Another pair of hands appear – gnarled and wrinkled with lots of brown age-spots.

I hear a voice call out "Granny, where shall we start?" Softly Granny is talking to the child whilst helping her to find the straight-edged pieces and corner pieces. I look at myself and see that I am bumpy all round so I know I may have a wait yet.

After a while, small fingers grab me and I hover over the jigsaw as the child tries to find a place for me. I see the picture from this viewpoint – it's a landscape with hills and trees, blue sky and clouds, grass and flowers.

Oh, I do hope I'm a flower – I love bright colours. Oh, I hope I'm a bright red or yellow flower. Come on, put me down there in the grass but by the road so that everyone will see me but all I'll have to do is blossom brightly and look up with a smile and bless the passers-by.

Oh, but I'm being placed somewhere else. Oh no, I'm going near the top of the picture, surely not a cloud or a plain piece of blue sky?

I'm snapped into place and I look around me at what looks like twigs. Oh no, I'm a twig – on a branch – on a tree – in a wood. What a tiny insignificant twig!

Oh, what a disappointment – I'm not going to be bright, I'm not going to be noticed or ahhhed over. I'm not even going to attract a bee or a ladybird.

A twig for goodness sake! A measly twig!!

But as I lay there on the jigsaw and the child and Granny go for tea, I question why I'm there and silent voices start to speak to me:-

A bright yellow flower looks up at me and moans "I can't see anything down here on the grass – you *are* lucky having a huge view of everything for miles around."

A dainty little bird lands on me and says thank you for giving him somewhere to rest on his journey south.

Another bird hops on and, as a tiny insect crawls over me, the bird gobbles it up and flies away satisfied.

An appreciative rambler walking by says to his friend, "Aren't these trees beautiful, every little twig contributes to its majestic shape."

A leaf on the end of my arm rustles contentedly as it imbibes the sap that is running through my veins.

A gentle breeze whispers as it passes, "Without you I would be silent – I love the noise you make as I blow through you. You are my voice that speaks of my presence."

A butterfly flits past, a bee hovers nearby, underneath me I can see all sorts of creatures sitting under my shade – of course I'm only a tiny part of that shade but they *are* using my little bit.

The longer I'm here and the older I get I see so much more that's around me and can tell what's going to happen as the seasons progress – my, I am getting knowledgeable!

I hear a whoop of joy and realise that the child and Granny have finished the jigsaw. They carefully pick it up to show someone else who has come into the room and see what the joy is all about.

There's a mirror on the wall and, blow me, I can see the reverse of the whole jigsaw. It's a blank! All the pieces look alike. None are better than the other but they fit together perfectly like a – well, a jigsaw!

Paul

When I saw you in the churchyard I formed a judgement there.
I thought you were a down and out, a little worse for wear.

And when you threw up on the grass what was I supposed to think?
The only thoughts that came to mind were – was it drugs or drink?

But then compassion flooded me. How could I help this soul?
But it was a secluded place – I felt so vulnerable.

It seemed more wise for me to pass by on the other side,
And so, unlike the Samaritan, my feelings I denied.

You came into the conference – have you made a mistake?
But no, you're clearly here to stay, and a front seat you do take!

It's coffee time, you're on your own, – you look so gaunt and pale,
I ask you if you're ok now – you're still a little frail.

My guilt is overwhelming me – I have to apologise.
You graciously accept, and smile, understanding in your eyes.

I share my picnic lunch with you – we cautiously converse,
But you aren't giving much away and I cannot coerce.

You may be a slave to drink or drugs or have cancer, AIDS or TB,
But I'll try to accept you as you are, – just as you've accepted me.

Life's Not a Box of Chocolates

Don't want a sickly strawberry cream
Or a toffee that makes my fillings loose.
I'll have a caramel hazelnut
Or Turkish Delight or chocolate mousse.

If only life was like a box
Of chocs that we're allowed to choose,
To discard all those painful times
And just ignore the Don'ts and Do's.

We could say no to all ill health,
Disablement and poverty.
We'd say "Yes please, I'll have that house
Complete with flowering cherry tree."

Don't want this marriage any more,
I'm going to throw it all away.
I'll pick a nice self-centred life
Where I can have all of my own way.

I'll not pick out the ones that ask
For me to go the extra mile.
Don't want rejection or abuse
Or any kind of hurtful trial.

How have our characters grown because
We've had to go through some nasty mess?
And if we'd had a magic wand
Would easy equal happiness?

And if we had the power to give
Everything for every request,
Would people be content with that?
Is that what they call "being blessed"?

Indian Summer

Approaching three score years and ten.
The Autumn of life so they say.
But not for me to accept the inevitable winter chill.
This is my Indian Summer.

The early morning stiffness is whispering
But I shout 'I can't hear you!'
I puff my way up the hill
But not for me the easy buggy ride.

The oblique rays of the sun still hold a warmth
And I turn my face to the positive.
I've ticked lots of boxes and worn the tee shirts
But there are more exciting days to come yet.

Recognise those shivers when the nip's in the air
But throw on a cardi and just go!
Push against the breeze of destiny
Delay its impending arrival?

It's Good to be Alive

It's good to be alive when the sun is shining down on me
Warming my skin so comfortingly.
The sea and sky so blue today
With silver slivers and white horses at play.
The grasses bend in the warm, gentle breeze
And colourful flowers seem to grow where they please.
Yes, I'm glad I'm alive to see this today.

It's good to be alive when nature's at its worst,
When lightning flashes and thunderclouds burst.
Rain like stair-rods entering every nook,
Or blanketing snow creating an Arctic look.
The sea-billows pound and rasp on the beach,
Spray flying everywhere, soaking all within reach.
Yes, I'm glad I'm alive to feel this day.

This Cat

Lazily stretching in the warm sunshine,
Eyes closed as if almost asleep,
But ears are twitching at every sound.
What is this cat hearing?

A seagull patters on the nearby tin roof.
One eye opens – how near is this bird?
A tail flickers – I *am* awake.
What is this cat seeing?

A breeze rustles the leaves on the path,
Pans clatter in the kitchen nearby,
A nose twitches – lips are licked.
What is this cat smelling?

A beetle scurries dangerously close,
Bees buzz over colourful flowers,
An ant crawls past an outstretched paw.
What is this cat thinking?

Familiar sounds – near and far,
Usual smells of his little world,
No competition today – no danger nearby.
What is this cat feeling?

Utter contentment!

Last Day on the Beach

The rhythmic whooshing of the surf
Slowly invades the nearby sand,
Unstoppable, untameable,
Pulled by a powerful unseen force.

Strident voices flowing over the airwaves;
Childish shrieks of unfettered joy;
Watchful gulls flying, hopeful of a meal
join in the cacophony.

Warm sand between the toes,
Gritty sand blowing into the sandwiches,
Damp sand being shaped into castles;
Wet sand moving further and further up the beach.

Warm sun, cool breeze,
Bright light, dark shade,
Last day of the school holidays,
Experiences, memories are made of these.

He's Late!

I look around to pass the time
but I'm in a nervous state.
I try to read a magazine
but I can't concentrate.

I check my watch and my diary
to confirm time and date.
I've got it right, I know I have
but he's now five minutes late.

I begin to sweat but it's not cold,
I'm really not feeling great.
I've got good reason to chicken out
'cause he's now ten minutes late.

I hear my name called out at last,
I jump and stand up straight.
I fumble with my coat and bag
'cause my dentist – he won't wait!

West Beach

Angular white sails gliding, sliding
effortlessly towards the yawning river mouth;
Buzzing little motor boats with a trailing white wake;
Calm sea shimmering, different shades of blue
glistening in the sunlight;
Tiny waves rippling at the water's edge;
Four legged friends splashing happily in the wavelets,
barking with delight;
Children jumping for joy, shrieking, screaming, such fun!
The monotonous drone of a distant aeroplane;
The anguished call of a lost seagull;
Snatches of conversation around me;
The plasticky thump of a beach ball;
The shout of frustration as the kick misses;
Pebbles rattling uncomfortably as they are being walked on;
The incongruous ring-tone of a mobile phone;
Parents shouting at unruly little ones;
Lovers laughing at a shared joke;
Families picnicking on a colourful sandy car rug;
Bathers struggling to change inside a beach towel;
Colourful kites soaring and dancing in the breeze;
Endless blue sky, stretching to infinity.
Tide retreating leaving rippled beige sand
lightening to white as it dries;
The gentle breeze passing by –
touching all – watching – listening – flowing – blowing
along the sun-warmed shore of Littlehampton's West Beach

Fingles Cave

Hear the deep wave approaching the rock –
Gathering momentum as it has travelled across the far ocean.
Louder – deeper – stronger –
Nearer it approaches.
Can you feel the impending excitement as it prepares itself
To crash upon the basalt columns of Staffa?
Hold your breath for a second or two then feel the great crescendo
As it spends all of its ocean's energy
In one great almighty crash upon solid rock.

Cymbals crashing – kettledrums banging – trumpets blaring.
Gulls screeching – sounds echoing into and out of the cave.
Back and forth – crashing and rumbling – spraying and fluming
Until the breath is all out.

And the sea starts to inhale once again,
Back into another breaker –
Back into the dark green depths
Ready to repeat the everlasting song of the deep
And the symphony of The Cave.

(Hebrides Overture, music by Felix Mendelssohn)

Seeking Peace

When the brain is racing with staccato shards
And emotions raging with thunderous fury –
When self-pity and hurting are jarring against the will
And unbidden thoughts intrude out of control -

Command them be still!
Rein in their waywardness!
Break their headstrong grip!
Tame their ferociousness!
Advance with your sharpened sword of peace!

Listen to nature's melodious songs
Of wood pigeon, song thrush, cuckoo and dove –
Imagine being lifted up on eagles' wings
And riding the thermals and soaring above.

Focus with gratitude on blessings received –
Things taken for granted that others may not have.
Remember precious times with loved ones who cared –
Those bright sunny memories that surely warm the heart.

Consider a way to give of yourself –
Plan helpful deeds to bring joy to someone.
Ponder some words that will lighten a load –
Then notice the peace that has crept into your soul.

Spare Parts – The Last Gift

I'm not myself today you know,
I've had another operation.
Part of me wore out last year
But surgeons told me not to fear
I'd be better for my next vacation.

I had a new kidney years ago
So now I can pee like a good'un,
But all the drugs and horrible stuff
Bloated me like a powder puff
And I'm left to look like a puddin'.

A cornea helped me to see my darling
Without a squint or glasses thick,
So I can drive my car once more
And see the view from shore to shore
And all those tiny boxes tick.

The bone marrow transplant made me feel
Just like the school gates' bright young mothers.
Invincible is my middle name
I'll shortly be in the hall of fame
As the oldest biddy with the bits of others.

But now, my love, you've gone to live
In that heavenly place above me.
You left me a gift as you prepared to depart,
My last operation – I have your heart
But you're no longer here to love me.

The Old Apple Tree

Green globes in clusters,
Bending branches towards the earth.
A hint of pink, a promise
Of a heavy harvest to come.

They wave in the wild winds
That dare the branches to break
But the tough old tree holds firm,
Just a few small fruit scatter on the soil beneath.

It stood firm in the frosty air,
Resolute in the winter rain,
Fragrant flowers bloomed in the sunny spring.
Now its ripening fruits are almost ready.

Out come the bags and boxes.
I gratefully pick the precious orbs,
Some for faithful friends and neighbours
Many for me and my larder.

Crunchy apple crumble, crispy apple pie and custard,
Tangy apple tart or just stewed with cinnamon.
Soft and spongy apple cake with cream.
Apples – picked with pleasure, eaten with joy – thank you old tree.

A Sense of Place

Inside a towering Swiss mountain,
Climbing up and up the rough hewn steps,
People overtaking, people coming down.
Sounds of children shrieking,
Sounds and glimpses of gushing waterfalls,
Cascades, torrents –
The sense of nature's unstoppable power.

Up, up, inside the lofty mountain,
Then suddenly, natural light
Far, far above me from an opening
In the top of the mountain.
I'm standing in a majestic cathedral
And the sense of almost silence envelops me.

The crowd has gone, I'm on my own
But, pervading the silence
Is the crashing of the water far below me.
I look up at the source of all this natural wonder –
The sparkling drops cascading from the hole above.

A shaft of sunlight bounces off the wet curtain
Creating an ethereal rainbow.
The celestial harmony reverberates around the cavern
And I experience a never-to-be-forgotten,
Overwhelming, awesome sense of place.

The First Snowfall

Adam stood upon the grass but couldn't understand
The strange white things that floated down and settled on his hand.

The sky was grey, air very cold, he saw but couldn't think.
He turned to Eve and said "What's this?" but Eve just stood and blinked.

They tried to catch the falling flakes but water they became.
They danced and waved their arms around and soon it was a game.

The cold flakes landed on their skin and melted in their sweat
But they began to shiver and their feet were very wet.

They covered up with animal skins but thought they'd never warm.
A wind sprung up and trees were bending – it was soon a storm.

Some hours passed by, the wind died down, they looked outside to see.
The ground was covered, white and cold, whatever could this be?

Life was going to be very hard, would anything out there grow?
This wasn't a paradise any more, now they've encountered snow.

A Late Spring Walk

The warming sun is turning up its heat as I explore the path
around the lake.
Through tunnels of bright rhododendrons, mauve and scarlet
and shocking pink.
I pause but, in the distance, more,
I'm drawn along by the urge to explore.
A fork in the path, I choose to go down to the lake,
Surrounded by reeds and tall grasses,
Yellow flags and dark undergrowth dotted with cow parsley.
A vista across the mirror-calm water, rippling as a breeze descends,
Bending just the top of beige-brown stems.
Another corner and a blinding surprise – a mass of colour
assaults my eyes.
Yellow and crimson and purple bright, I stop a moment to appreciate.
I sit for a while on a fallen log that is carved into a natural seat.
There's a cooling breeze as I rest my feet.
I study reflections of yonder bushes and trees
And hear a woodpecker "knocking his knees".
On through the shade I follow the path, through mighty oaks
and silver birch.
A small pond – so still – where dragonflies dart
Birdsong all around – a choir in a woodland church.
Young rhododendrons dotted here and there
And huge fallen trees, rotting homes for the bugs.
A young rabbit scuttles off, a squirrel runs alongside me,
intent on his quest.
Trickling water somewhere near on its way to the lake.
A sudden open sunny glade with molehills all over
With tiny blue and yellow flowers and wild purple clover.
Back along the path, dappling sun and shade, unfurling ferns,

Wicked brambles and spiky teasels.
A glimpse of that squirrel again in the tree –
I think he's playing catch-up with me.
Another glimpse of the lake near the bridge where my walk will end,
At least for today.
A pair of swans go sailing by and geese are honking on yonder bank.
I've seen this woodland trail with Autumn-gold leaves falling
like pennies
And in Spring and Summer green, in the heat and the rain.
No matter when I visit, it uplifts my spirit
And ensures that I'll want to come back again.

(The Lake at Ashburnham, East Sussex)

An Acquired Taste

I have a friend who's very much the opposite of me
So when she shows me things she's bought she'd like some flattery.

But I can't lie and say it's great when really it is not
So I have to think of other words so I don't say "What rot!".

"What do you think of my striped settee with its cushions
of leopard spots?"
"It's very unusual" I slowly say as I look at the little dots.

Her new drapes have ties of something that looks like worn out
bits of string.
I struggle but I can only choke "Well if you like that sort of thing".

The new dress comes out, she obviously wants a great big compliment
But all I can manage is an encouraging noise and
"That's certainly different".

The orange bag to match the fuchsia suit for her imminent vacation?
I'm striving but I can only say "That's an interesting combination".

She's covered a wall with African masks that she must have bought
in haste.
Once again I'm trying not to offend – "That's an acquired taste".

But when it comes to my birthday and she's bought a beautiful plate,
I open my eyes and my mouth in surprise,
"I really like that, thanks, it's great".

Ashes to Ashes

The scrapyard beckoned the mighty train in nineteen sixty-eight,
But a man paid three thousand pounds for it and saved it from its fate.

It was the Flying Scotsman, an iconic beast of steam.
To see it pass or ride aboard was every schoolboy's dream.

When diesel and electric trains were new kids on the block,
Lumbering engines were cast aside with all their rolling stock.

But Alan Pegler saved it and, despite the rising cost
It was restored and sped again so the icon was not lost.

Now Alan's gone but his ashes were kept to make his wish come true.
They're being put in the firebox by his daughter and the crew.

So, if you see the Flying Scot on its tribute journey to York
Just give three cheers as it passes by and old Alan goes up in smoke.

That First Day

After winter snow and springtime frosts,
When that nip in the air chills the bones,
Today, feel the warmth from a southern breeze
Blowing up from the tropical zones.

No matter the date, or what flowers are out,
If the calendar still says mid-spring,
To me, it's the first day of garden delight
That only warm weather can bring.

The red of the tulips is startlingly bright
And the bluebells are brilliantly blue.
The sun brings them out like nothing else can,
That first day of a beautiful view.

I know I'll have to weed and prune
And the lawn will need a regular mow,
But as I inspect last year's delights –
The green shoots are starting to grow.

The seagulls are screeching and traffic is humming
But I feel so satisfied,
'Cause this is the very first day that I
Can sit in my garden outside.

The Day We Went to Leonardslea

We're going out – let's cheer and shout, we're off in the car and we agree.
I've got the map upon my lap, we're going off to Leonardslea.

The gardens beckon but I didn't reckon we'd drive with such hilarity.
So there we sat with laugh and chat,
we've missed the turn to Leonardslea,

Who gives a toss, we came across a nice place for a cup of tea.
After our delay we asked the way and soon we came upon Leonardslea,

Well, some paths were steep and I fell in a heap
and lost all pride and dignity.
I gave a yelp and someone helped me back on my feet with dexterity.

Our way we did make down to the lake where a dog is splashing happily,
But it gave us a look then came and shook
and wetted us from chest to knee.

When we finished our browse amongst the flowers,
we thought we'd have a nice cream tea.
We looked for a scone but the last one's gone, never mind,
the cake smells deliciously.

Last on the list, we nearly missed The Dolls House,
we've just got time to see.
Then back to the car to ooh and aah 'bout our lovely day at Leonardslea.

The Somme – 1st July 1916

Here am I at thirty-five
Wondering who is left alive.
All day long I've heard the guns
Aimed at all us British Sons.
Who is left there to survive?

I'm trying to bring the rations up.
They'll need some bread and tea to sup,
But they've been gone so very long,
It may have gone so horribly wrong.
I'm thinking they've been "sold a pup".

When I arrive I start to gag,
I've just looked down at a body bag.
There's not much left of that young squaddie,
His life has gone – he's just a body.
We ought to wrap him in our flag.

I shouldn't look, I feel so sick,
The smell is bad, the air is thick.
There's a bloody leg still in its boot
And a hand with a gun he's tried to shoot.
O Lord, I hope his death was quick.

I fought in the Boer War when I was eighteen
And when you're so young you're bound to be keen,
But the enemy here isn't taking no quarter,
These boys are just sent like lambs to the slaughter.
I don't think I'll ever forget this scene.

I can't do nought but stand and cry,
Why did so many men have to die?
How did it all get so out of hand?
Will future generations understand?
Will they remember the first of July?

Possible thoughts of my Grandfather, James White,
15 December 1881 – 25 June 1965,
1st Battalion East Yorkshire Regiment who was awarded the DCM
for "showing great courage and devotion to duty in bringing up
rations to his company under very heavy shell fire"...
He couldn't ever speak about what he'd seen.

Marked for Life

I seem to have a lot of marks that tell of various things
That happened to me long ago, aside from sprains and stings.

The tiny craters from Chicken Pox and the dog bite on my hand
Are marks from childhood when I was too young to understand.

The motorcycle exhaust pipe which burnt into my flesh
When as a daring teenager, was a mark of carelessness.

The deep cut through my thumb was when I smashed a china plate
Which left for evermore a mark that showed my anger was so great.

The stretch marks of my pregnancies, those little silver lines
I wore as marks of pride because they were of happy times.

Trying to open a sardine can is something so hard to master
And doing it impatiently leaves marks of that disaster.

An operation on my spine was a scary time of life
And the scar it left showed the skill and the mark
of the clever surgeon's knife.

When I slipped on the wet kitchen floor and landed flat on my palm
It left me with a little lump, the mark from a broken arm.

The scratches from cats, barbed wire and brambles
and other times of strife
Are mingled with wrinkles and laughter lines that are my marks of life.

Something Strange

What was that noise I heard
As I lay in my cosy bed?
Should I go and explore in the dark
Or just turn the light on instead?

What was that passed by my side
As I sat watching my old TV?
I turn round to look but it's gone,
There's just nothing there to see.

I'm just walking quietly along
And I hear someone call out my name.
I look round to see who is there
But there's no-one I can blame.

One day in my house alone
And facing the kitchen sink,
Behind me, a spoon in a mug
Gave a sudden and very loud clink.

I watched as the bathroom loo roll
Unwound right down to the floor
Then the shower utensil pole
Crashed down on the thick glass door

Now I wonder if my house is haunted,
Coincidence or imagination?
I'm not going to worry because
There's probably a good explanation.

Ammerdown

Retreating to a quiet place, in the grounds of a country house, surrounded
By parkland and woods and gardens in which to read, write, wander and relax.
So, off to the woods with brolly and shoes for the wet,
A carrier bag to sit on a log and a camera to capture a surprise.

So I was inspired – inspired to write
Of the sights and sounds of the woods.

Another day to explore the grounds but nearer the country house;
Long wet grass, orchids and clover, and trees with interesting shiny bark.
I came across an overgrown lake with yellow irises and reeds
With swifts darting around catching their daily dinner.

So I was inspired – inspired to write
Of the solitude and peace of the pond.

Another time in the topiary, the formal clipped yew and box.
In and out, up to the orangery with the view that Lutyens had created.
By the cascading white Philadelphus, a man appeared,
and we talked of plants and peace and ponds.
"Are you the gardener?" I asked without thought. "No, I live here"
the owner of the big house replied!

So I was inspired – inspired to write
Of the hedges and flowers of the garden.

Last day outside in the sun with sketchpad to capture the converted stable block,
The archway where horses had clattered with their carriages,
The chapel, the labyrinth, the inviting table and chairs under the shade of the tree.
The fragrant lavender, the sweet roses, the tinkling sound of a water feature.

So I was inspired – inspired to draw
Of the visible history where I'd retreated away.

(Ammerdown House, a retreat centre in Wiltshire)

Foolish, Fearless or Fun?

So, who doesn't do foolish things?
Surely everyone can think of something?
That time when you embarrassed yourself
But maybe others were admiring your nerve.

Foolish things on holiday were when I went 'off piste'
And nearly missed the waiting coach
But what a memory I have now,
That sight that no-one else saw.

But was I fearless? – pushing myself
To do what I would do if I were young?
And where does fear of man come in
To stop me from having some fun?

Standing up in front of a crowd
With walking stick and baseball cap –
I really don't care what people think
As I do my 'Granny Rap'.

When I was young, with no confidence
I must've missed out on loads of stuff,
I wasn't as pretty as the girl next door
And I thought I wasn't clever enough.

I wouldn't say boo to a goose.
Maybe I didn't have a mind of my own,
But now I'm not scared to stand up for myself.
I now know the right words and the right tone.

So now when I'm faced with a choice
And I think, now is that foolish or brave?
I get a little nudge at the back of my mind –
I can't do this stuff in the grave!

We Had to Flee

It was not safe for us any more,
To stay in the land of our birth.
The death threats were real, we feared for our lives
And how much is a baby's life worth?

So my little family packed our bags –
Just took what we could carry.
We said goodbye to those who could stay,
We didn't dare to tarry.

Our hearts were heavy, we didn't speak much,
Even our baby was quiet.
The days were so hot but we needed our coats
'Cause the cold was so dreadful at night.

It didn't take long for the blisters to burst,
And our backs were aching real bad.
Our tummies were rumbling, we sometimes felt sick
But we'd eaten all the food that we had.

We'd been given some gifts when our baby was born
So we sold them to pay for supplies,
And even though we were quite naïve
We learnt by mistakes to be wise.

People took advantage of us
But we just kept plodding on
Until one day we felt we could stop,
That the threat of danger had gone.

So we've paused a while in a far-off land
And we think of the babes who've been slain,
But one day we'll return to the land of our birth
When it's safe to go home again.

(Thoughts of Mary, Joseph and baby Jesus – or any refugees)

The Magical Misty Moment

I wandered o'er the moors and hills to where the land
gave way to a hollow
And where the streams of water led and gave the desire just to follow.

And so I went down and stood by the edge of the quiet water
and listened awhile
To the distant noises of birds and sheep that gave me pleasure
and made me smile.

But then a mist rolled down from the hills and covered the scene
in front of me
Until all was muffled and silent and still and time became an eternity.

I knew there was water in front of my feet and grass behind me
where I stood
Transfixed, spellbound, as life had stopped and made me feel
I'd turned to wood.

Helpless and blind and deaf, it seemed I would have to wait
for the mist to clear
If I was to move from this very strange place and out
of the magical atmosphere.

A gentle splash, I was not alone and a whirr of wings around my head
Told me something else was as lost as I but he was a-wing
and now he had fled.

I could do nothing but sit on the ground and feel the texture
of the tussock grass
And wait for a breeze that would surely come and the magical misty
moment would pass.

Suddenly I was aware of something, breathing just behind my neck
And, petrified, I sat stock still as my body became a wobbly wreck.

I couldn't move forward because of the lake but now the breathing's on my hair
It was something big and it was sniffing around, I have to move but do I dare?

I slowly stood and turned around to see a mass in front of me
And as I peered I caught my breathe, a stag, as big as big could be.

Then as we stared, both breathing hard, and peering as the light was dim,
He nudged me, blinked, and turned his head, he wanted me to follow him.

The stag was huge with antlers vast but as I gently touched his cheek
He turned and slowly led me off, away from the edge of the murky creek.

Then up on higher ground the mist thinned out, dissolved completely, then
He sniffed my face and trotted off, he'd gone – my Angel of the Glen.

The Long, Long Wait

Have you ever sat for three hours on a stationery plane?
Well this we did at Gatwick whilst watching all the rain.

We should have landed at Edinburgh an hour and a half ago
But here we sit so patiently, just 'going with the flow'.

Some men who gave up waiting decided to 'up and go'
But we are on our holiday so our spirits are not low.

We breakfasted at 4am and now it's ten past eleven
So all our tummies are rumbling and a boiled sweet tastes like heaven!

If we had got the car out we'd have all been there by now
But to drive through all the thunderstorms – there might have been a row!

We just have to hope the coach will wait for us at the other end
But I think there's quite a crowd of us that the company's trying to send.

Of course it could be far, far worse – we have a decent loo
And drinks of water passing round and some of us are laughing too.

I've read half of my book already that I have brought from home
But now I'm getting really bored – I think I'll write a poem.

We've had a lot of excuses – plane mended but papers not there,
The weather, a strike and now we've heard there's been a hand-grenade scare!

How many times have I looked at my watch? The hands don't move very fast.
Hang on – the captain's talking now. It's time to go – at last!

Circles of My Life

I don't remember my teething ring
But I'm sure I must've had one.
I do remember that many a year
I sucked my right-hand thumb.

When I was five I was dressed in white
And sparkly angel wings,
And a wire halo encircled my head
As I joined nativity kings.

Made daisy chains to wear on my wrist
As I was too young for bling
Then plastic bangles and hula hoops
And necklaces made of string.

Then one remarkable day I wore
A golden wedding band
And over the many years to come
More gems on the other hand.

Now, getting older, the circles are
More under my fading eyes.
But no-one sees the sexy garters
Circling round my thighs!

V.E. Day Celebrations

What a wonderful day it was! They sang and drank and danced because
They'd had enough of war and fear.
Now it was over – a time of joy, for man and woman, girl and boy
To soak up the rapturous atmosphere.

Among the crowd with tear in eye were those who'd had to say
"Goodbye"
But hadn't welcomed home again
The loved ones, captured, missing, dead – all remembered with poppies red,
But what was lost was for our gain.

Yes, *all* would celebrate V.E. Day, no matter what sad hearts did say.
They toasted Churchill and the friendly Yanks.
They bopped and boogied and let down their hair, at Buckingham
Palace threw hats in the air,
For they had freedom and they gave thanks.

Now 75 years since that first V.E. Day, whether a quiet or loud display,
Whether a private drink or a public ball,
No matter our colour, religion or race, we still celebrate peace in this place
And we'll treasure what that means to us all.

The Hard Climb

Of course I'll do it, I'll climb that cliff.
I'm sure it's not that tough,
But it doesn't take long to be panting hard.
I just don't have the puff.

With walking stick in one hand,
The other's pulling on the rail.
My son is pushing from behind.
I'm determined not to fail.

After many, many, many stops
To catch my breath again,
I reach the very, very top
And I didn't need a crane.

My calves may ache like mad tomorrow
But I have reached the summit.
I'll have a sense of achievement
And proudly say "I've done it!"

The Year 2016

That was the year that shocked the world,
Well some of it anyway,
When every adult in two great lands
Were allowed to have their say.

The Referendum in the UK
Gave us all the chance to choose:
To stay in the European Union
Or make shock headline news.

So "Brexiteers" were leavers now,
"Remainers" choose to stay
Cameron was so convinced that it
Would easily go his way.

Debates, discussions and arguments,
Adverts on lorries and bus.
Remainers spoke of doom and gloom
The leavers thought it a 'plus'.

So, with thousands spent and tempers frayed,
Friends and families split in half,
We were all agog when the great day dawned –
Who would have the last laugh?

It was a shock – the world had changed.
Britain had had its say.
But it would take years to know who was wise
On Britain's "Independence Day".

But over the 'pond' was another big vote
When Americans had *their* say.
The rich and poor turned out to choose
The President of the USA.

Again the polls predicted that
Safe Clinton would win by far.
The alternative was unthinkable,
The Trump was too bizarre.

He'd build a wall round Mexico,
He'd boot all Muslims out.
His radical talk lit a people's fire,
That certain result was in doubt.

Then the shock – the Trump has won!
The world is reeling once more.
Democracy's great – the majority wins,
But what's the future got in store?

So how have these two momentous events
Finished up such a surprise?
Were people so fed up with how things were?
Thought nobody heard their cries?

And what will it do to the rest of the world?
Will there be a domino effect?
One day the history books will show
If our world is strengthened or wrecked.

Our Daily Gift

Every four years we're given a gift
But no-one says "Thank you".
It's an extra day at the end of Feb
Because of a second or two.

But no-one 'leaps' or jumps for joy
Unless a lady proposed,
Then it's a ring and a bunch of flowers
And cheers as the champagne flowed.

So does the 29th of Feb
Just pass at a dizzy rate?
Or are we grateful for every day,
No matter what the date?

Listen to Your Heart

Words can hurt but don't let them imprison you.
Listen to your heart and be free to be yourself.

Negativity can bring you down if you let it,
Listen to your heart and rise above it.

"What's that awful noise?" – Go, sing like a bird!
"Mutton dressed as lamb" – No, bright colours are what you are!

"You can't, you're no good at words" – Go, write that poem or book!
"You shouldn't even try" – Go, see if *you can*!

"You're bound to fail" – At least you'll have tried!
"You don't know how to converse" – Go, talk to that neighbour!

"You're not clever enough" – Go, join an evening class!
"You'll not understand" – Go, listen to that lecture!

"You'll look silly" – Just dance your heart out!
"You can't do that at your age" – Try and see if you're able!

"Your bum looks big in that" – Who cares? And why?
"You'll get hurt" – Sometimes you have to take a risk!

So who puts you down? What fears hold you back?
Listen to your heart and you'll not live with regrets.

Fox in the Garden

Two ears prick up, you've heard me near.
Have I invaded your secret space?
Two eyes light up, maybe full of fear.
Did you think this was the safest place?

Are you curled up tight thinking I can't see
Your gold-brown body lying there?
You're quivering, are you about to flee
Off to your dark and cosy lair?

Your eyes half close, more sleepy than scared,
Perhaps you sense I'm not a threat.
Do you know I just want to stand and stare
And imagine you as my private pet?

I drink my fill of this beautiful sight
Knowing one of us soon has to move away.
Then, ending this moment of pure delight
I backwards creep. Little fox, come again one day.

The Oyster Pond

Circle of murky water but glittering in the sun.
Algae floating aimlessly amid ripples blown by the breeze.

Blue and yellow pedaloes with knees a-bobbing as they go
With white froth a-trailing behind their flow.

Lots of children shouting, and laughing, full of joy.
To be out of school, out of the house, it's freedom they enjoy.

Gulls are a-wheeling, eyes searching for discarded food.
Union Jacks a-waving, bare branches only just stirring.

A queue of cars along the road, a line of people on the river-walk.
Sun beating down and burning my knees, I think Summer's trying to come.

But clouds appearing cover the sun and a chilly breeze cools my face,
Reminds me Spring is clinging on but the Pond is still a nice place.

Memories of Lake Garda

Don't you just love travelling, especially by air.
You get up at the crack of dawn, "I've had no sleep" you swear.

The nerves kick in as departure time approaches much too fast.
You packed the night before of course but the list is oh so vast.

You're off – you look for Just You tags, you wonder if you'll fit;
Will they all be as daft as you? Of course they will you twit.

The lovely Xenia herds us all until we're like her flock.
She dashes about like a collie dog but dressed in a swirly frock.

So – boats didn't sail on the day they should; hotel meals were 'odd',
No one knew what 'smooth-hound' meant, was it really cod?

Eating the pasta we'd seen being formed, oh what a row we made!
Learning all about a violin then listening as it was played.

In a couple of places we needed the loo but it was a hole in the ground!
For those whose thighs weren't very strong, well, we didn't hang around.

We had olive tastings and ferry rides, one to a beautiful Isle
where we had wine and nibbles, now that's what I call style.

The Limoncello drinks were nice, the guide was tasty too!
The time is rushing by us now, the week is nearly through.

Some had drinks at The Grand Hotel, bet the waiter thought
we were a rabble
And instead of just a hole in the ground the loos were all in marble!

The long hot walk to the Roman Palace – the market – the ferries – the sun –
The birthday bash for some of our 'gals' – the poetry, laughter and fun.

    Some brave souls went up a hill then flew off over the town,
    Trevor hired a sensible bike, others just sat and went brown.

The airport looms for our journey home – of course there's a short delay.
    I wonder if we'll meet up again on a Just You holiday?

My Little Bit of Heaven

Yes, nearer my God to Thee, am I in my longed-for garden.
I make myself sit, with a cup of tea, to look and enjoy, be satisfied and be grateful.
I didn't have a lawn before, well only in the early days
When football and flowers didn't mix.
Then shingle which looked lovely at first
But how I missed the softness and green.
Now the expanse is peppered with daisies and dandelions and mess,
but it's mostly green – and soft.

There's snails and slugs and brambles and weeds
But also hardy flowers and shrubs.
The colours amaze and a few smell nice
And I love putting things in tubs.
The bees and butterflies delight themselves in the blossom,
Goldfinches, sparrows and blue tits all love the food we put out
Greedy, raucous starlings squabble and squawk but they all keep the garden alive.
And, without much help it seems like most things thrive!

From early Spring when the first snowdrops show,
Through primroses, daffodils and tulips galore.
Bluebells and celandines then forget-me-nots
All do their thing – I just watch – in awe.
Through Summer's heatwaves, downpours and gales
To Autumns fading beauty when sadness overcomes me,
I'm so alive in my garden – I'm living the dream.
My little bit of heaven – 'til the real thing comes along.

Other People's Words

Some words just roll around the tongue
And can be called delicious,
But sometimes just a phrase we hear
Seems almost too fictitious.

That child, who missed the butterfly
That floated past like fluff,
Was really miffed because he said
"My eyes weren't quick enough."

"The border is plangent with colour"
Said Monty Don on TV,
And a happy chap said "Someone's
Just lit a match inside me."

A phrase that made me think a lot –
In fact I found I was wallowing –
Was written somewhere on a wall,
"Leave footprints worth following".

Again on TV the lady on the train
As homeward from holiday they sped,
Was muttering to her patient man
"Be nice to get back to our own bed".

"I kept getting a crick in me neck
With all those pillows" she said.
I smiled and wondered why she hadn't
Just taken them off the bed.

I smiled some more and chuckled a bit
As her thoughts just tumbled free.
I knew how she felt when she finally said
"I'm desperate for a wee!"

The Unprovable

Is it out there somewhere, in the air?
Or is it imaginary, in my head?
Our feelings just aren't tangible
And you can't touch something you've just said.

So you hear sounds that I can't hear
And I have visions you can't see.
We doubt ourselves but does it matter?
I believe you and you believe me.

So is the mind the same as the brain?
And what's the cause of the aching throb?
I think I'm sane but what does it matter?
It's just a chemical electrical blob.

Strange things happen, we can't explain,
Co-incidence or E.S.P?
Is there a time warp from long ago?
Is there a dimension we can't see?

What about our beating heart?
The source of love or an electrical pump?
We have emotions that make us cry
And we have shocks that make us jump.

Are there angels around, unseen?
That feather – that chill of air upon the skin?
The unseen hand that held us back,
That faint sound of a celestial hymn?

Is there another world out there
That sometimes merges with our own?
And will we all be there one day
And realise that we have flown?

Our Town

Buzzing jet-skis churning up the river;
A power boat speeding and roaring like a lion;
Large yachts, small craft, with flags a-fluttering;
Queues outside cafes; chips a-frying;
Gazebos struggling in the riverside wind;
People with dogs and bikes in the fray;
Megaphones, laughter, all having fun;
That's our town on Waterfront Day.

Darkness has fallen, the procession begins;
Torches are blazing, the bands go before
Decorated lorries, colourful costumes;
Red Indians, Elizabethans and Supermen galore;
Children are dancing high up on their float;
Crowds lining the streets cheer with delight;
Down to the bonfire and fireworks they go;
That's our town on Bonfire Night.

Sparkling displays and glittering lights;
Decorated tree by the town centre clock;
A manger with Jesus and Mary and Joe;
Wise men and shepherds and a small woolly flock;
Christians are singing their carols aloud;
Stalls overflowing with gifts sublime;
Music and laughter and kids having fun;
That's our town at Christmas time.

The Blob

If you go down to the beach today you're sure of a big surprise,
'Cos I went Thursday, saw a blob of jelly – with great big staring eyes!

The council came to the beach later on – they meant to take it away.
They thought it was dead, but it gave a blink,
and they all moved further away.

The RSPCA came to the beach, poured water over the blob,
It made a pitiful wailing noise and someone started to sob.

A man from the local aquarium came to the beach with a tank
But when he saw the size of the blob, his face was a total blank.

Some children came to the beach yesterday,
the blob didn't scare them a jot.
They prodded and poked and bullied the thing, but did it move?
It did not.

An engineer dug a trench from the sea, up to the blob, with the hope
That an incoming tide would take it away, down the slippery slope.

Now if you go down to the beach today, you'll join the crowd
and the queue,
'Cos the blob has reached the edge of the surf and I'm sure it's wailing
"Thank you".

Where to Go

I'm trying to decide what to do 'bout a holiday week or two.
Do I go on my own and just take a phone,
Or is there a friend who is 'blue'?

So now, is it here or abroad and how much can I really afford?
The brochures are tempting but my mind is emptying –
Oh, what a smorgasbord

Do I want to laze on the sand and get hot and over-tanned,
And burn my ears? I'd be bored to tears.
No, that stuff I cannot stand.

Now a cruise on river or sea might provide variety,
But I cannot control when my stomach might roll
So I think that's not for me.

Could I climb a mountain high and try to reach for the sky?
But I pant and puff when the going gets tough
No, I'm not fit and spry.

Now I love a turquoise lake sipping wine and eating cake,
So, where's a scene I haven't been?
That sounds an ideal break.

But what if the weather is stormy? the thought is starting to floor me.
My son says "Just go – you'll be fine – I know"
"Alexa – will you decide for me?"

One Shop Wonder

Whatever the size of your village or town,
Banks and Post Offices are closing down.

But people who don't have transport are cross
With the decision makers who don't give a toss.

So someone's decided to merge the two
To halve the rent and double the queue.

Now what can others incorporate
To bring their customers through the gate?

Could the greengrocers merge with a butcher's shop?
'Cause the veggies make stew with a nice lamb chop.

Or could fishmongers make more cash
Selling spuds to make fish pie and mash?

Could a haberdasher merge with a pharmacy?
'Cause a pricked finger will need some TCP.

A milliner's and a vintner's are fine
To wear a big hat and try a new wine.

A furniture shop in a library
To read a good book on a nice settee?

So why has no-one thought of this spoof
And put all these outlets under one roof?

Oh silly me! There's lots of stores,
It's called a supermarket of course!

May Day in Lydney Park

The daffs are over and tulips past their best
but the primulas flower with delight.
The heather has spread, with its myriad pink dots
and there's a shrub with drooping sprays of white.

The man on the yellow mower's been busy
so the smell of cut grass fills the air.
Fortunately, he's left the old daffs to die down
like a border of unruly hair.

The three-tiered fountain is splashing away
and rippling the water all round.
There's nine or ten seats just for people like me
to sit and relax with the sound.

Rose bushes are leafing and preparing to bud
and the soil's dug and raked but not wet.
There's a World War I garden with black metal men
and we vow we will never forget.

The hard landscaping round the pond is in stone,
and in layers for different views.
Bordering the lot are trees of many shapes
and textures and heights and hues.

I come to this place once or twice in the year
when I visit my loved ones again.
I wonder what flowers will be out,
after months of warm sunshine and rain.

(This poem is etched into a big stone in Lydney Park)

Nature's Worst

Dismal dullness, creeping darkness, grey clouds deepening,
gloomy half-light,
Misty drizzle, hair a-frizzle, spits and spots, drips and drops.

Sprinkling, dribbling, trickling, running, falling faster, tipping, gushing,
Dollops dropping, thunder rumbling, clouds are emptying,
bursting, tumbling.

Stair rods straight and cats and dogs, deluge, flooding, paths awash.
Wind is strengthening, trees are bowing, branches breaking,
wires howling.

Lightning flashing, thunder roaring, devils screaming, shrieking, wailing.
Tin rooves flying, fences crashing, rivers rising, overflowing.

Roads are torrents, gutters spilling, gardens swamping,
plants are drowning.
Sandbags drenched like heavy sponges, soggy, sodden, waterlogging.

Storm is passing, wind is dropping, sky is brightening,
clouds are whitening,
Rain is easing, sun is peeping, raindrops glistening, heart is lightening.

The Kitchen Waltz

I wanted to make a couple of cakes and be alone to concentrate
But hubby wanted to make his lunch so decisions had to be made.

Who goes first? Who should wait? Was one more urgent than t'other?
We sort of had a compromise and our ingredients we did gather.

So, him to the fridge while I'm at the sink then, doing a 'pas a double'
Him to the cooker, I get my scales, we pass in the middle so nobly.

We're watching each other's whereabouts, our brains working overtime,
While cutting, buttering or weighing out, oh the movements
are sublime!

Over the floor we glide with ease, in the middle we blow a kiss.
Anything sharp is kept point down so a mess we manage to miss.

Worktop to oven, cupboard to sink, one two, one two, three four.
We could have done with music as we crossed the kitchen floor.

So, cake's in the oven, lunch on the plate and coffee is in the cup,
But will we be so harmonious when it comes to the washing up?

Choices

I can't control who loves me or decisions that they make.
I can't do nought about my height nor rectify past mistakes.
I can't make others treat me right nor make them nice and kind.
I can't insist they come with me if they want to be left behind.

I cannot change my skin colour or affect the type of weather.
I can't decide what day to die – I'm not going to live forever!
But there's a lot that I can do and decisions I can make,
How I respond to challenges and pathways I should take.

I can control how hard I work and how I spend free time.
I can decide to push myself and what mountains I should climb.
I choose to be accountable and respect opinions of others.
I can apologise for myself and forgive my sisters and brothers.

I can choose to try again and forgive myself for failing.
I'll try to be more positive – no more moans or wailing.
If I think first, I can control the words I need to say,
And whatever life looks like right now – I'll choose to enjoy today!

Hot Summer

Crispy, crunchy, crackling under sweaty, sandaled feet.
There's been no rain for such a long time.
No green underfoot just robust, yellow weeds
Flowers are now struggling – gone past their prime.

Crispy, curling leaves of brown
On stressed shrubs and thirsty trees.
Gasping for air in the thick humidity,
Facing the direction of the slightest breeze.

Dark clouds approaching, it's gone very quiet.
Where are the birds? We don't hear a tweet.
Flashes then rumbles, oh please let it rain.
We all need refreshment and respite from heat.

At last the sky opens, pitter patter at first
Then splashing and pounding, it hurtles hell for leather.
The waiting is over, it's throwing it down.
Oh don't we just love our great British weather!

The White Walk

The cloudy sky grew darker and the day gave way to the night
And I hunkered down with dinner before my fire bright.

I heard the wind a-howling as I pulled my curtains closed
And with a full-up tummy I comfortably dozed.

When curtains opened in the morn, a sight before my eyes –
The world was white and oh so still – a beautiful surprise.

After breakfast, suitably dressed in wellies, hat and scarf
I ventured forth into the snow and up the garden path.

The air was still, my breath came out like a dragon's smoky plume
As I clumped and stumped along the way before I got my broom.

But that can wait, 'cause I cannot – my need to wander grows.
I'm being lured out to the trees by loudly cawing crows.

The gate won't budge so I climb over – landing in a heap.
A friendly robin comes to laugh – well, gave a happy cheep.

The snow's so soft for every step, yet crunches deliciously.
All sounds muffled in the quiet wood as I go from tree to tree.

The sudden flutter of wings above and I'm sprayed with snow from a twig
And white-edged branches rigid and stiff have never looked so big.

I stand quite still to take it in, I strain my ears to hear
And nature whispers all around – a spiritual atmosphere.

Retracing steps with frozen toes, only my footprints on show.
Can't believe how long I've been crunching around in the snow.

Back in the warm, think – crumpets, butter and maybe cake to follow.
I hope it doesn't thaw tonight so I can do it again tomorrow.

Little Boy Jonathan

There once was a lad called Little Boy Jonathan.
Jonathan rose above the teasing about his height because he was kind.

Kind thoughts and soft words eventually got him many friends.
Friends became colleagues as he rose through the ranks to become 'the boss'.

The Boss was well thought of because he saw the best in everyone.
Everyone was happy until the country suffered 'economic problems'.

Problems became wage-freezes, then wage-cuts and times became really tough.
Tough people started complaining very loudly to Jonathan.

Jonathan used his savings so he could pay his people.
People rioted below his office window and someone threw a brick.

A brick hit Jonathan hard on his head and he fell, forever, down.
Down below there was a deafening silence as they realised their kind boss had gone.

Gone was the boss, gone was the factory, gone were their jobs.
Jobs they'd all enjoyed, been paid for, that fed their families.

Families who didn't know what they'd got until it had gone for good.
Good folks never die in people's memories.

Memories of Jonathan lived on for many generations.
Generations to come tried to emulate the man they called
Big Boss Jonathan.

On Eagles' Wings

The bright, hot day fills the senses
With woody perfume and nature smells.
I've walked through the waving corn
Then climbed the hill midst sweet harebells.

Ascending higher up the crags,
Clattering stones break under my feet,
'Til I reach the place at last
Where my handsome, feathered friend I meet.

He quivers at my approach
And spreads his wings and lowers his back.
I mount and grasp his shoulders
And we alight the rocky stack.

The thermals lift us high
Above the patchwork quilt below,
Through cool and misty cloud
Where I see the rainbow colours glow.

A sudden, churning swoop
And downward like a thunderbolt.
The lake approaching fast
And then a shocking, jarring jolt.

His talons grab a fish
Then mighty muscles fly us high.
The lake receding fast,
I can't help letting out a cry.

Exhilaration and joy
As I share the mighty eagle's flight.
We're soaring, climbing high
From deep, dark lake to mountain height.

We land upon the crag.
I slide from shiny, shimmering wings.
I leave him to his supper.
My heart is glad and my soul sings.

Through The Old Wooden Door

Wandering off the beaten track where I hadn't been before
I came across some undergrowth with a battered wooden door.

Ivy was dripping from over the top and weeds were almost knee high
But it beckoned me strongly to come up close and the urge I couldn't deny.

The hinges were rusty and so was the bolt, the iron ring cold to the touch
But I couldn't manage to open it, I was shaking much too much.

I looked around to see if there was a parapet or wall
From a manor house or ancient church or big baronial hall.

But there was nothing to give a clue of the old door's history
And I shivered as I felt caught up in an ancient mystery.

What was on the other side of that battered wooden door?
Would it matter if I just took a peep? Was I breaking any law?

What if I was transported to another time or place
And found myself with Vikings or floating around in space?

Maybe there's a secret garden like in the book I read,
With beautiful flowers and lush green grass and robins around my head.

My curiosity got the better of me and I grasped the iron ring
And as it turned it gave a click and a metallic sort of ring.

With bits of ivy stroking my face I pushed against the wood
It gave a little and creaked a lot, I pushed as hard as I could.

I stared at the sight in front of me, it was empty, bare and stark
And I realised I was at the end of a Sainsbury's car park!

My Russian Dolls

Mama Harriet worked in a circus, had nine children in a row.
She stitched and sewed the costumes for many a glittering show.

Mama Millie came out of her, a clever seamstress too.
Made clothes for all and sundry and four children as they grew.

My Mama Dora sewed as well, but just for her and me,
'Cause she had time for hobbies – sold her paintings for a fee.

Now I am Mama Pauline but I have to buck the trend
For I have two boy children and the line of Mamas ends.

A Stroll in the Late Spring Sun at Ferring Rife

Strolling in the sun by a lazy little stream – time to look around and enjoy nature and the changing season.

Trees in the distance, sun shining on their golden-brown branches – remnants of an autumn splendour.

Puffy, white clouds overhead ballooning in an expanse of ultramarine.

White, fluffy and bobbly bulrushes with brittle, white stems like poor man's candyfloss. No longer the proud brown sentinels of last year.

Bare willow tree with thick trunks sprouting twiggy branches like a surprised haircut – had a bad hair day! All reflected in sky-blue water.

The dark fir tree also reflected with a rim of straw reeds like a whiskery chin.

Beige reed grasses bending – all facing the same way.

A hedge of pale dead grass interspersed with hoops of green and burgundy giant brambles with thick, fierce thorns.

Shallow ponds edged with squidgy mud and spongy grass, dotted with small islands of spent plants.

A thatched roof and red brick chimneys peeping between small trees, tall trees, dark green fir trees.

Fences and stiles covered in silver-grey lichen, sprouting like ragged, papery oak leaves.

Lines of erect white stalks like soldiers with bayonets uplifted.

Seems like all has died – but –

New life is sprouting on dead-looking branches – catkins, soft pussy willow, seed bunches pecked by young blue tits darting hither and thither.

Flashes of fading yellow daffodils, small clumps clinging on to early spring.

Patches of clear water with healthy green growth swimming and swaying with the ripples. Big, succulent oval buds – shiny and sticky-looking in the sun.

A small weir with sudsy white water and bubbles sailing downstream.

A narrow pathway, edged with new green leaves and flanked by a hedge of still bare brambles, the path mysteriously disappearing round a corner under an archway of small trees

Suddenly a blaze of early bluebells nodding in the sun, flower petals unfurling in the unexpected warmth.

The quack of a duck giving away its hiding place in a dense thicket over a small rivulet – his glossy, deep turquoise head and neck shimmering in a small spot of sunshine.

A blanket of lime green algae but with fresh green flags poking out defiantly – a promise of colour to come.

Life and death all around – mixed together.

But the dead will fall and rot and be covered with new life.

Life's overcoming the dead – new replacing old.

Winter's going – Summer's coming. Inevitably – predictably – thankfully.

Going Sunbathing

The kids have gone to school,
The washing-up's been done,
I've made my bed and the cat's been fed
Now I'm going to laze in the sun.

I get my bikinis out,
Now which one shall I wear?
I try them out and prance about,
Oh why am I shaped like a pear?

Then on with suntan lotion,
Now where's my old straw hat?
I've got a good book and the phone's off the hook
'Cause I haven't got time to chat.

I carry my deckchair out
Then bring it in again,
I just can't win, the sun's gone in
And it's pouring down with rain.

Willpower

(or the losing battle)

How I'd like a nice sticky bun
But my diet's just begun.
I'm stuck with my lettuce
'Cause my old man's just bet us
A couple of bob when I've won.

I've said "I'll do it begorrer
No more cups of sugar I'll borrer"
But to hell with my hips
I must have some chips,
P'raps I'll start on my diet tomorrer!

(apologies for grammar!)

Irritations

Why is it whenever I wash my hair somebody calls at the door?
And why, whenever I visit the loo do I get phone calls galore?

Why, when the floor has just been washed does the kitten do a puddle?
And why, when the cupboard's been tidied up do I find it in a muddle?

Why, when I put on nice clean sheets does a nosebleed seem to happen?
And why, when I've done up a parcel neat somebody tears the wrapping?

Why, when a pile of washing's been done do the heavens open up?
And why, when I get my best china out does somebody break a cup?

Why, when the carpet's just been swept does the parrot chuck out his seeds?
And why, when I want to laze in the sun do I notice all the weeds?

Why, when my best TV programme's on do visitors choose to call?
And why, when the children play outside do they ask me
to look for their ball?

Why, when I'm just dropping off to sleep does my husband
start to snore?
And why, when I take a drink to bed do I spill it on the floor?

Why do these things always happen to me? Is there any way to stop it?
But when I have time to contemplate, I guess I wouldn't swap it.

It's nice to be in such demand, of that I have no doubt.
'Cause if my life was dull and quiet I'd have nothing to write about!

Me and the Spider

The other day whilst kneeling down
Upon my kitchen floor,
I came upon a spider
With hairy legs galore.

Now I hate creepy-crawlies,
They really terrify me
And this was no exception
As it tried to slither by me.

I looked at him and he looked at me,
The hairs rose on my neck.
I quietly had hysterics
And kept my screams in check.

But as we sat there staring
A look came to his eye
And I felt a stab of pity,
He was far more scared than I.

My trembling stopped, I felt quite calm,
My tum no longer queasy.
Him so small and me so big
I could've squashed him easy.

I backed away across the floor
I knew I couldn't hurt him,
He gave me such a grateful look
Then scurried off under the skirting.

Depreciation

I'm going out for my daily stroll but I don't have a destination.
It's just to move my creaking joints and prevent that operation.

Now do I need my trolley today or my stick on this occasion?
I think I'll leave my purse behind in case there's an altercation.

My glasses are on, my teeth are in, I've put on my embrocation.
I've got a little bottle of juice in case of dehydration.

The road is fairly busy today, I need all my concentration.
I know I'm getting in the way of the younger generation.

A man's approaching, a skin-head type with a very fierce-looking alsatian.
Do I stand quite still? Avoid its eyes? Oh I'm feeling some aggravation.

Phew, he's passed, I don't need to fret, it's a minor irritation.
Someone else is approaching, to my left or right?
Oh just give me some indication!

I'm puffing my way up this hill today, think I need some oxygenation.
Getting slower and slower, feel I could sleep. It's definitely depreciation.

Oh no, my Nora Batty stockings are dropping,
I can feel the sliding sensation.
I need to find a nearby seat 'cause I'm walking like some old crustacean.

Right I've had a good rest but I'm needing the loo
'cause I'm getting a slight inclination.
I'm walking home quicker than on the way out
'cause I've got some real motivation.

At last, in my bathroom I look in the mirror but that causes
consternation,
I've been in the street with my curlers in! So much for my organisation.

What to Eat?

I'm thinking of making a nice meat pie
with gravy and chicken or beef
But then I think of the pastry
and decide on a lettuce leaf.

Now what about an entree
or tasty fishy starter
But then I think of the sauces
and decide on a little 'tomata'

Should I make a dish with pasta
or brown and healthy rice?
Or can I concoct something
with a thin cucumber slice?

I could make a stew in a little round dish
and a light puff pastry bonnet
But getting out the butter dish
I see something's growing on it!

I look in my fridge for some cabbage
but I'm too late, it's gone all yellowy
I'm getting desperate now so
I'm glad there's a nice stick of celery!

(written for my Weightwatchers' class)

Growing Old Dis-gracefully

"Don't judge a book by its cover"
I heard a gentleman say.
He wasn't meaning me of course
But it made me think all day.

The young folk may look at my wrinkles
And the colour and state of my hair,
And when they've just looked right through me
Do they think "there's nothing in there"?

Well, inside I'm young and I'm daring,
Who cares what anyone thinks?
I may look sedate or schoolmarmish,
But in my head I'm still a little minx!

As the quantity of years remaining
Diminish with every birthday,
The quality's getting more important,
To enjoy whatever comes my way.

I've found the company's crucial –
Fun people bring joy to my life.
They stimulate brain cells to work, 'cause
I'm not always sharp as a knife.

By balancing the safe and the sensible
I ask "What's to lose any more?"
I'll appreciate all and live life to the full
And load good memories into my store.

Maybe one day when I can't do much
And I'm reduced to eating soft eggs
I'll remember and laugh at those hilarious days
'Til the tears run down my legs....

The Picnic

We went for a picnic the other day 'cause the forecast said 'It's fine!
I bought all the food and all the right stuff,
  it was going to be a wonderful time!

  The car ride was lovely, though Johnny was sick,
    but I managed to clean my dress
And when he shut his thumb in the door it was only a bit of a mess.

  Well we found the right spot and the blanket came out
    and the mould didn't smell all that vile
  When Dad's chair collapsed and his fingers got trapped
    he only swore for a while.

I emptied the hamper, put food on the plates, was busy making a brew
But Granny was having a choking fit – her face had gone all blue.

    Young Johnny had picked up a hard-boiled egg
      but it rolled off down the slope,
Midges were biting, wasps on the cake but I wasn't giving up hope!

  Grandpop's broken a champagne glass and badly cut his hand,
There's blood all over the tablecloth – it's not going quite as planned.

    It's time to go home but poor Johnny had slipped
      into a big pool of slime.
  We're smelly, we're bleeding, we're bitten, we're cross,
    but oh what a memorable time!

The Shower Pole

We bought a contraption the other day but we had to assemble the thing.
Oh, there were instructions on paper alright
and we didn't need hammers or string.

We counted the parts and laid them all out,
they're numbered and pictured as well.
Looks easy we thought – how hard could it be?
We've made things before – can't you tell?

But no – it wasn't as easy as that. Does this bit go outside or in?
The arrows and numbers don't seem to make sense,
it doesn't do what it says on the tin.

It seems to say 'turn upside down' for this bit but then the spring falls out.
The rubber washer was so tight that it snapped.
Now we're beginning to shout.

So, what's this bit for? It just doesn't say. I think it turns and locks.
We ought to have a coffee break and think outside the box.

Refreshed and calm we look again, perhaps we need brute force.
This plastic bit is upside down. Keeps the water out – of course!

We should have threaded the baskets through before we joined it all
So, take it all to bits again but try not to let it fall.

It looks OK so we each take an end and manoeuvre it into the shower.
With one of us balancing on some steps we discover it should be lower!

So, we shorten and lengthen at least three more times until we got it just right.
The spring has got a mind of its own but at least it holds it tight.

So, when anyone stays and uses our shower and admires our piece of work,
We shrug and we say 'easy-peasy' of course,
as we look at each other and smirk.

Poppy Poo

I had a little cat who I called Poppy Poo
And she was so attached to me she stuck to me like glue.

She draped around my shoulders or she sat upon my head
And curled up on my chest or back, when I laid down in bed.

She cried to come out shopping so, upon my shoulder sat
And I tied her lead around my neck, and my cheek she'd gently pat.

She then decided she would sit up high upon my noddle
And had to cling on tightly so that she didn't wobble.

Sometimes she'd face behind me with her tail around my nose
Another time she'd sit up straight in a proper haughty pose.

If someone walked towards me looking sadly at the ground
I'd stop in front, so they looked up and a smile broke from their frown.

Everybody loved my cat and she loved the attention,
They told their friends of Poppy Poo – I didn't get a mention.

People cooed and petted her and took photos all the time.
They took a lot of videos and put her into rhyme.

One winter's day we went outside, she loved the falling flakes,
She also kept my head real warm, I was like a toasted cake.

When we got home, I put her down but she didn't move or purr –
She'd frozen solid in a ball, cold ice upon her fur.

I said goodbye so quietly and had a little cry
And put her in her basket by a lovely blazing fire.

When I awoke from the nearby chair she wasn't in her bed.
I screamed and heard a purring noise that came from on my head!

So now when we go out for walks, I put her in my trolley,
She's zipped up tight with her head poking out and looking very jolly.

Embarrassment

Have you ever been embarrassed, when you think you'll die of shame?
Or watched in horror as someone else's face just turns to flame?

Well, the other day I went out of the house and felt something strange in my jeans.
I pulled out my pants from the night before and hoped nobody else had seen!

I remember a friend going up on a stage but she had just been to the loo
So, her skirt was tucked into one leg of her knicks and everyone had a great view!

In a plush, blue-carpeted theatre foyer, and heading to the stairs,
I noticed lots of bits of white were following me everywhere -

My sandals were disintegrating and great chunks came off the sole
The horror turned to laughter as, barefoot, I tried to stroll.

Somewhere in France, in a hotel room, I decided a bath I would take
But smooth sides meant I couldn't get out, it was nearly my biggest mistake -

I had to let all the water out, twist sharply to retrieve the towel,
Kneel on all fours and despite cramp, climb out,
but boy was my language foul!

Half way through another posh 'do' with dignitaries bejewelled somewhat,
I'm told I've dribbled chocolate sauce down the front of my very posh top.

Oh, memories are coming thick and fast of the times I've felt a fool,
With the jumper put on inside out I didn't look so cool.

Odd socks; odd gloves; a pulled thread caught on a button;
Food smeared all over my cheek – I must've looked like a glutton.

And have you ever been seated on a wet ledge or shelf?
It really looks and feels bad, as if you've wet yourself.

I wore a little mini skirt but my tights had a ladder at the knee
One stoop and it's a hole that everyone can see.

I can't be the only one that remembers embarrassing times
So, tell me yours and we'll laugh together and make up lots of rhymes.

My Initial Thought

What's this on the BBC? Trump has now got BSE?
Heard it from the BMA, now all over the USA.
It couldn't be from KFC, they spray all theirs with DDT.

Now what's this on ITV? There's a leak from the KGB?
Putin's now got RSI, so he's off for an MRI.
His rival's killed by a JCB? His tombstone reads just RIP.
Was he a PLC or an LTD? Oh no that might be the MCC.

Just listened on my MP3 to a very old song by 10CC.
Do you remember ELO? Well now it's all about J Lo.
Was she once after rapper Jay Zee? Or was that Mel B or C?

I've now heard that the GPO just got a call from a UFO!
OMG it's a bit OTT, better check with the RAC.
They came out in a big SUV and said there's a fault – call BT.

They've told me to contact my MP – well he's a bit of a VIP,
But he shouldn't have got an MBE – he was caught wrapped up in PVC.

Oh dear, I'm trying to find our NHS? Look it up with GPS?
My head is spinning, think it's PTSD – goodbye, I'm off to A and E.
(Or should that be my GP?)

Junk Mail

Oh goody, the postman's been, I think, as something's come through the door.
But no, it's just more pesky flyers that have fallen on the floor.

Now what are they telling me that I need? What do they advertise?
It's double glazing on windows new. Now isn't that a surprise!

There's one for up-and-over doors that my garage's already got.
A new boiler that I just don't need, or servicing – on the spot.

Lawnmowing? Weeding? It says good rates. A man to fell my trees.
A lady to clean my house for me – does she get down on her knees?

Window cleaning – oven cleaning, should I be taking the hint?
This one offers an eyesight test. Yes, by now I'm starting to squint.

Van and two men, they might come in handy. There's guttering and roofing repairs.
A decorator and handyman and lovely reclining chairs.

I could go on, and on, and on 'cause the pile I've got is growing.
One day I'll test their sincerity – I'll call them out when it's snowing!

Underthings

There was a young man from Zaire
Who wanted some new underwear.
He just could not choose
Between tight or loose
So decided he'd look at a pair.

The shopkeeper said that to model
A pair of Y-fronts was a doddle.
Up and down he did strut
And showed off his butt
And said "This is how you would waddle"

"I don't want to waddle" he said
"I want to look sexy in bed"
So the Boxers he bought
As they were less taut
And certain things didn't feel dead.

Now his girlfriend who lived nearby
Was questioning what she should buy.
So asked the shop girl
To give her a twirl
In something she'd wear for her guy.

"Does madam want Bloomers this size?
Is there something you want to disguise?
See how they hide
Whatever's inside,
And they cover my thunder-thighs!"

"Oh no, I'm really not big,
In fact I'm as thin as a twig,
So Briefs I will buy
To show off my thigh.
I'm sure he won't give a fig".

So come the great night of their date
Their desire to undress was so great,
They couldn't care less
About the state of their dress
Admiration of undies could wait.

The Passenger

I gave a lift to someone in my car the other day.
I was happy and contented, said he didn't have to pay.
I knew the route to take so we're on our merry way…
Until….

He cleared his throat and said to me "D'you know the Highway Code?
'Cause you're clearly going faster than you should along this road."
Well, shocked, I couldn't answer him – I'm still in happy mode…
Until….

"Mind that child over there and watch out for that chap!
This isn't the way I go to town, have you got a map?"
My dander's rising, getting cross, I think I'm going to snap…
Until….

He shrieks at me to stop the car, he needs a nearby loo.
Why didn't he go before he left or is this something new?
I'm getting quite impatient now, I'm sure my face is blue…
And then….

"Oh no, a false alarm" he says, "just carry on a-going".
I rev quite loudly and I'm puffing and I'm blowing.
He's tapping feet and fingers as the traffic starts a-slowing…
And then….

"Can't you overtake this lot?" he shouts into my ear.
The air around is crackling, a nasty atmosphere.
"It would be quicker walking – you're still in second gear!" …
And then….

"That's it, I'm getting out" he says in middle of the street.
I didn't know he was so agile and so nimble on his feet.
I let him go and sped away – oh isn't silence sweet! ...
But....

In my mirror I could see him slumping to the ground
And out of nowhere, pity and compassion I have found.
I might be like him one day so I slowly turn around,
And then – he saw me – and smiled....

A Safari Story

Whilst on a safari years ago, in a land rover, with a guide,
we'd gone to look for elephants, so big and dignified.

We drove along, all happy and glad, 'til our guide stopped with a jerk,
he'd needed to 'go' behind a bush and we sat there with a smirk.

Well, suddenly, in front of us stood the biggest bull elephant ever, and
his rumbling noises got louder as we all huddled up together.

Should we jump into the driving seat and try to reverse the car?
Or fire a gun? Or shout like mad? Or anything more bizarre?

I suddenly felt I should join our guide, bent down behind a bush,
but the elephant just inched closer and used its trunk to give us a push.

Someone screamed and someone cried – it could've well been me.
The trumpeting started, all hell let loose, he's as angry as could be.

Where is our guide? Should we jump out and run?
But where would we run to? What if we're all turned upside down?
Someone – what should we do?

All of a sudden there's a tinkling noise -it's coming from my pocket.
My mobile's ringing but my hands are shaking and I'm just unable to stop it.

However, the elephant stops its charge, it's not heard this noise before.
It swings its trunk and rumbles low and just seems very unsure.

I manage to get my mobile out and held it out in front.
The elephant flapped its ears a bit and gave a little grunt.

Then it turned and ambled away – it doesn't like my ringtone.
Unbelievably that great big lump is scared of my mobile phone!

Gone Fishing

When I was young, in the countryside, I fished in a stream
with a stick and bent pin.
I don't remember what I caught but it probably fitted in a very small tin.

So, when I joined a friend by a river, a bigger stick and pin I bought.
With our sandwiches and thermos flask, I looked forward
to seeing what I caught.

Well, first up was a size 6 trainer, on its own – not much use,
Then up came a plastic bottle but it wasn't filled with orange juice.

The fish didn't seem to want to bite, not even a tiddler for my jar.
Then, hey, there's something on my line – for goodness sake
it's a giant bra!

Now who would've left that in the river? My mind is boggling
at the thought,
But the line is bending once again, oh no, a bicycle tyre I've caught!

My friend's hooked a fish but threw it back in, and now my line
is taut again.
Whatever it is it's very big, I might have to go and hire a crane.

I'm sure the line is going to break, the rod is almost bent over double.
The two of us reel and pull like mad, I'm sure it's going to be
worth the trouble.

I think it might be a river shark, my friend is laughing,
"Don't be a wally",
But it appears we're in for a shock – it's only a rusty shopping trolley!

Dangerwoman

On my round, delivering leaflets and things, I often have a surprise.
Some things are good, some things are bad, some funny in my eyes.

For instance, at one door, I heard a girl singing out of tune,
But when she saw me, she cried out "My baby's coming soon!"

Another lady asked me in to pin up the hem of her dress.
Well, what could I say? For a cup of tea and a biscuit I said "Yes".

Now, making people jump out of their skins, I seem to have the knack.
Unfortunately, more than one old dear has had a heart attack.

One day I came across a child quite firmly stuck up a tree.
I spread my arms, told him to jump – alas, he broke his knee.

One lady, expecting the vicar for tea, was highly disappointed.
I said "I'm sorry but it's just me, I'm not the Lord's anointed".

One gent saw me coming and opened the door but I saw the glint in his eyes,
So, when he lunged, I raised my knee quick – boy, did he get a surprise!

Now I'm not a danger to anyone, a jinx or a walking threat
But I'll not poke anything through your door
'cause you've got a dangerous pet!

The Woolly Coffins

Our Gran and Grandad died last week,
might have been what they'd been scoffin'.
The funeral chores were down to me so I had to choose their coffins.
Well, Granny was a knitting champ so I thought it would be quite apt
To make a couple of woolly shrouds that would match her latest hat.
So, Grandad had a Fair Isle one, but chunky, with navy twirls
But Granny liked her twinsets 'plain' but wearing 'stockings' and 'purls'.
Now, flame retardant wool's no good if it's going to be a cremation,
But what if it rains and it shrinks to their shape before final disintegration?
Of course, they could go baggy and saggy and grow to twice their size.
I've got to decide what to risk – we don't want a nasty surprise.
Come the big day and we're all in 'rows', wondering what
might be the glitches
But the vicar knew some funny tales and had us all in 'stitches'.
He talked about the 'pattern' of life but as I continued to sit
I thought about my new business name –
"Knit Your Granny a Coffin Kit"
Just as I thought it was going well, my heart did a massive flip –
I noticed a strand of wool had caught on a nearby pallbearer's zip.
Just then those woolly lumps did move, down the ramp they slowly travelled
So, we all sat and watched in horror as both coffins they unravelled.
As their feet came into view, complete with bunions and corn
I gasped as I thought they might be naked as the day that they were born.
As Grandad showed his knobbly knees, I managed to break the thread
And I noticed that the man with the zip had turned three shades of red.
Meanwhile, the vicar covered them with the skimpy altar cloth
And we all breathed a sigh of relief as they went –
they've finally been 'cast off'!

How Did We Manage?

Before we had a mobile which we use to text our home
We had a square of Bakelite that we called our landline phone.

A biro or a ballpoint pen is convenient I think –
Took over from the fountain pen that covered me with ink.

The ten shilling note bought a heck of a lot and seemed a fortune to me
But it went the way of a lot of things and the coin's worth just 50p.

The old cash register is obsolete, replaced by a digital till
So, whatever you buy in whatever shop you'll get a digital bill.

How I loved my record player and my dozens of 45's,
The hours that I could rock n' roll or a lively twist or jive.

Our digital hearing aids are a boon instead of a metal trumpet
Now heart problems have a pacemaker instead of having to lump it.

Electric razors, toothbrushes and clocks and now an electric car,
Artificial Intelligence, Alexa is bizarre.

How did we manage all those years ago? Were we always so contented?
We have to embrace new technology 'til the next thing's been invented.

The young grab hold of everything new, some think the old aren't worth it.
Well, this old silver head's part way there when I switch on and surf it!

The Gremlin in the Oven

In my oven a creature lives,
Can't see it but I know it's there.
He's the reason my baking fails.
It's totally him, I swear!

For example, my Victoria Sponge,
A simple recipe to follow,
But when I take it out of course,
In the middle – a definite hollow!

Meringues go in, peaks all spikey,
Meringues come out, totally flat.
I tried a souffle once, but after,
I could see where the Gremlin sat!

In go chocolate brownies – mmmm,
Out come chocolate blackies – ohhhhh,
I know he turned the temperature up
Even the smoke had a devilish glow!

A frozen ready meal fares no better,
The middle is always cold,
And what does he do to my biscuits
That should come out all gold?

Now no-one else has a Gremlin
As far as I can see,
So do I have to humble myself
And admit it's all down to me?

Just a Check-up

Went to the dentist the other day,
Just for a check-up you understand.
He was very sorry for the delay
But I saw the tooth marks on his hand!

I wasn't worried as I laid back,
Even when I thought he would tip me off.
But my nose had an itch then a tickle in my throat
Then I heard his big sigh as I started to cough.

The bib's round my neck and he's peering so close
I can see all the pimples on forehead and chin.
I try not to look but the hair in his nose
Is making me start to giggle within.

I close my eyes quickly and open my mouth.
He prods at each filling to see if it's tight,
But I hear a ping as one flies out it's hole,
I groan as I know my forthcoming plight.

He says he's got time to fill it right now,
I say, "Oh just do it, it's got to be done".
So, in go the pillows of white cotton wool
And I spy the needle and think 'Oh what fun.'

I'm sure it's not working, I can feel everything.
My lip is squashed between my tooth and his thumb.
The road drill is pounding and so is my head
But fortunately now my whole mouth has gone numb.

The drill starts to scream and the water just spurts
   Then trickles icily down past my neck.
He stops and suggests that I rinse out my mouth.
   My jaw's just got stuck. I feel a right wreck.

Now how can I sip when my lips have gone dead?
The pink stuff goes everywhere, not much goes in.
   Back on the couch I open again,
   He puffs it all dry, let the filling begin.

He pushes and shoves til amalgam's in place
   And smooths and tidies this fang of mine.
The bib comes off, the couch shoots up
   I try to get off, think I've broken my spine.

"All done" he trills as he opens the door
"See you next year" with a smile just like frost.
But the nightmare continues as I go to the desk
And they show me just how much it has cost.

Groundwater Day

I bought a lovely modern house in Littlehampton town.
'Twas on the west side of the river, that jewel in their crown.

The deeds did show a great big wall would save me from high tide
And great big banks surrounded houses on the other side.

Unlike a lot of neighbours who had rented out their pads
I lived here like a local and thought what I could add.

Deciding on a goldfish pond I started digging down
But water started seeping in – a very murky brown.

I didn't lay a membrane 'cause the hole was filling fast
But as I watched – it wouldn't stop and o'er the top it passed.

Oh heck, the water's past my knees – I don't know what to do
And now the wife is calling out – "It's coming up the loo!"

I've heard the Civic group had tried to warn the Council Planners
But I guess they thought that they knew best
'cause they hung out lots of banners.

Well now I'm neck-deep in this mess I wonder who I'll sue,
I've tried to ring but no-one's there – have they *all* gone for a brew?

I'm standing here like the boy at the dyke but I haven't got a plug.
It's turned into the West Beach Lake and I am…glug, glug, glug!

Standing in an English Queue

Post Office, supermarket, bank or boutique,
I just hate standing in a queue
Is it because I'm already stressed?
Or because I don't know what to do?

I'm OK with an orderly line
Properly marked out where to stand
Where we all know our allotted place
And we all think "Ain't life grand"

But, if someone, without an "Excuse me"
Cuts in front, like some people do,
Do we mutter, or grumble or shout or shove,
Or think, 'they just don't know how the English queue.'

What if the queue isn't straight as a die?
What if folk move out of line?
What if they don't move forward in turn?
I know I'm stressed, I'm losing my mind.

We grin and bear it when, down the line
Someone is saving someone else's place.
We do it ourselves so we try to appear
That we don't mind, we're full of grace.

Now what tops the lot in the queuing game
Is standing in line and you're needing the loo
You think you might just make it in time
But then you realise you're in the wrong queue.
AAAAgh!

The Perfect Cake

I wanted to make a special cake for a Macmillan Coffee day.
It had to be a signature one with a pretty flag display.

A picture showed a chocolate one with three or four layers of sponge
But I wasn't sure I could go that high without it starting to plunge.

I've made lots of cakes before you know but I thought I'd try a new mix
So I read it right through several times so I wouldn't get in a fix.

Only slightly different from my usual one, I wouldn't get in a stew,
Just a bigger tin, cook it whole then, when cold, just cut in two.

So the day before the coffee morn, I measured, mixed and baked.
I set the timer for forty minutes, I mustn't make a mistake.

Then taking it carefully out I saw it start to wobble like jelly
So back in for another ten – it doesn't do that on the telly!

Out it came and I tested with a skewer just like I should
So I let it stand within the tin. My! it's really smelling good!

Two minutes later I happened to look at how it's starting to cool
But it was slowly sinking into a gooey chocolate pool.

I turned it upside down upon the proper cooling rack
But it started sinking the other way – it's squeezing through the cracks!

So I turned it over once again and left it on a plate,
I can't do anything now so, just leave it to its fate.

So now it's cold what can I do? I'll cut the middle out.
My husband ate it for his pud, "It's lovely" he did shout.

Now, to slice it in half I try but without a middle – not easy.
I lift the top – it breaks in half – I'm getting very greasy.

So, fudge icing over the bottom halves, whipped cream upon the top,
Squeeze the semi circles together – no-one will notice my flop.

Fill the hole with strawberries, hang the flags across the break
And everyone said "What a clever girl to make such a perfect cake!"

Sticky Stuff

Wrapping a parcel? How hard can that be? Just scissors and sticky tape!
You fold paper round and hold it on top, the start of a very good shape.

The problem arises when you need another hand
'cause you can't cut the tape with just one
Unless it's fixed firmly to table or chair, then half the battle is won.

So, let's start again with both hands this time
and cut the sticky tape first.
Attach little bits to the edge of the chair and try very hard not to curse.

So, wrap the paper around again, hold firmly with one hand,
Reach for the sticky tape on the chair – it's going just as planned

Oh no, it's not as easy as that – I've leant against the cuttings.
I use my nail but they're squashed quite flat.
Now I'm doing more than tutting!

With gritted teeth I try again, paper and tape are ready.
I've just got to hold the paper still and STICKY – TAPE – STEADY.

No! No! No! No! The paper's moved, the tape has stuck all wrong
I pull it but it makes a hole! The sticky's just too strong!

Patch up the hole – use a paperweight, don't let the tape go slack.
It's covered in fluff but I don't care, I think I've got the knack!

The parcel's wrapped – it's fairly neat, I'm feeling satisfied,
But then – oh no – I can't believe I've left the price on inside!

The Silent Hour

For sixty minutes I try to sit and focus on God alone.
Not to sing and not to, oh, did I switch off my mobile phone?

Behind me I hear heavy breathing, I think it's only a dog.
Now concentrate, I'm sure He'll speak (God, not the dog!)
but my mind is like a fog.

I thank, I praise, (all in my head), I wonder if I'm mumbling.
But no, it's coming from over there, an empty tummy rumbling.

What were those words I read just now that I can't get outa my head?
"Live adventurously" Yes, There's a lot to do before I'm dead.

I ponder about the choices I make with the gifts God's given to me
But then someone stands up to speak,
think I heard the crack of his knee.

Eyes closed again I ponder anew, should I ask God what to say?
I inwardly chuckle as unbidden thoughts come rapidly winging my way.

A lady stands and asks for prayer for her brother's very ill.
I focus again and pray peace for him for I know that's in God's will.

My back is getting mighty stiff, my bottom's gone all numb,
I clench my cheeks and stretch my toes, I *must not* twiddle my thumb!

I surreptitiously glance at my watch, it's past my coffee time.

As if to say "I heard that thought" church bells begin to chime.

I focus once again but, no, the holiness has gone,
I'm thinking of Mary Berry now and how she made her scone!

Someone's speaking to end the meeting, eyes open, stretch and cough.
Ah, They're bringing trays of coffee round and a special cake to scoff.

Time to Waste

I want to communicate, so now
I have to decide which phone.
My mobile's handy but the land-line's free,
These decisions make me groan.

I choose the mobile but, more decisions,
Shall I call or shall I text?
Decide to call but the battery's flat,
So I have to decide – what next?

The land-line's fine – dial the number,
Engaged's the tone I hear.
I wait a while then try again,
I'm through! I give a cheer!

I listen to the opening spiel,
There's options one to ten,
But I'm not sure which one to press
So, I listen to the menu again.

Surely there's a human there
With whom I can just speak?
But I've hesitated far too long
And it's cut me off with a squeak!

I try again and eventually get
A person on the line,
But she has to put me through again
To option number nine.

But option nine is busy so
I listen to a tune.
Ah, Greensleeves, yes, I know this one
So, I begin to croon.

Well, when it's played about four times
I hear a voice again,
But it just says there's no-one there,
I've done *all* this in vain!

Walkies

Today I decided that, now, my pet was that age to walk,
So out of the door we went – just me and my lump of pork.

"Lump of pork?" I hear you ask. "You don't mean your Sunday joint?"
Oh, don't be so daft my friend, 'tis my Vietnamese pot-bellied oink!

Yes, I took my pig out today, he's got his very own lead,
But oh the trouble he caused as he took off with remarkable speed.

Yes, he pulled me quickly along and I could hardly keep pace.
Then a cat appeared on the scene that Porkie decided to chase.

Down the road we flew at great speed 'til the cat went in
somebody's garden,
But as Porkie trashed all the flowers it was me that said
"Beg your pardon".

Porkie calmed when the cat disappeared and I thought to go home
would be best
But a lady was coming along with a chihuahua clasped to her chest.

Have you ever seen a chihuahua leap out of an old lady's grasp?
I'm afraid I just burst out laughing as she sunk to the ground
with a gasp.

Now I'm in an awful dilemma, do I try to catch her dog?
Or shall I help her to her feet or chase my fleeing hog?

I'm sorry folks, I didn't do what I really should have done.
I saw my Porkie down the road and decided I should run.

Well, he was trotting much too fast but then he screeched to a stop.
I wondered "What's caught his eye?" It was a butcher's shop.

He stared at a hanging carcase and sausages draped on the slab.
He made no attempt to flee as his lead I went to grab.

Now Porkie turned to face me with a fearful look in his eye
And he meekly walked back home as I whispered to him "pork pie!"

Woolacombe Beach on a Summer's Day

I looked down upon thousands of ants. Oh no, they're people, thronging the enormous beach, from dunes to surf as far as I can see.

Negotiating our way over thick yellow sand, sucking me in up to my ankles, calf muscles protesting as we look for a family-size space amid the brightly coloured tents and neon-stripy windbreaks.
Aha, a plot for us, surrounded by said tents and windbreaks – ah well, I can just see the water in the distance.

Chairs settled, mats laid, shoes off, baseball hats on. Rummage in bags, towels pulled out, flasks uncupped, lunch box opened – tuck in. Squawk – oh – forgot about the seagulls – on Lydia's head, lunging for her sandwich – missed! We cup our hands over every following morsel.

Toilets needed – oh when can we just sit and relax? Waddle back through the thick sand, queue oh so politely, make a note of where the ice cream kiosks are, waddle back again.

At last, time to look around at the multi-coloured kites, toddlers with their pink buckets, orange spades, bright green beach balls accidentally landing on oily, pink, prone people, brown bikini bodies and taut, tanned torsos, and me with all my clothes on.

Far away, over the top of the windbreaks, across an expanse of greeny-blue sea is a hazy mauve lump called Lundy Island – possibly not so crowded as here!

Tide's coming in, surf's coming up, crowds are retreating back. Will the dry bit of sand accommodate all those ants? It's already covered with soggy towels, gritty blankets, squashed sandcastles, heaps with just a head and shoulders peeping out, shoes and socks scattered, kiddies' abandoned surfboards.

Suddenly I notice people leaving, Kiosks closing up, hoards heading for the hot tin can bin, sorry, I mean car park – must be tea time and we're going with the flow – hope there's a chippy on the way home!

Incensed or What?

'Twas serious and solemn in the church that day
And the vicar was facing his flock,
Then, far at the back, the choir processed forth,
Each one in their flowing white frock.

The verger was swinging the censer about
And the smoke was filling the aisle.
The choir was chanting, the flock joining in
And each face wore a curious smile.

The smiles became giggles as the smoke wafted through
But the folk at the front wore a frown.
Then uproarious laughter from those in the fog
And folk started falling around.

The vicar thought "Crikey – has revival broken out?
But I haven't yet preached my sermon!
Are they slain in the Spirit? I can't see through the murk,
But I'm sure the verger is squirming."

By now some are holding their throats and they're wearing
An agonising expression.
There's coughing and wheezing mixed in with the laughter,
But that's only the start of the session.

The censer is dropped and the coals all fall out
And set fire to a chorister's dress.
Well some handy holy water is saving the day
But oh what a terrible mess!

They never did find out who swapped the incense
For a secret ingredient,
But no-one complained, and more came the next week
Just in case there was more 'happy hemp'.

Don't Let the Biscuits Bully You

What do you do when a bully
Tries to make you give in?
Do you say "Oh all right – just one"
Or determine that he won't win?

What do you think when some toffees
Look so appealing at you?
Do you think of the taste in your mouth
Or picture your teeth stuck like glue?

When, on your own, and you're tempted
And a friend texts "Are you being good?"
Do you think 'she can't see, she won't know'
Or go, brush your teeth like you should?

So don't be a victim to bullies
Like crisps and biscuits and snacks.
Say "No I won't. You can't make me!"
And go, pat yourself on your back!

(Another one at Weightwatchers)

Jammy Days

Oh I'm a little stripy wasp off out to look around.
What can I see, what can I smell as I hover near the ground?

There's lots of pretty flowers which waft their scent my way
But I'm bored with all the usual stuff that I did yesterday.

I don't have many enemies 'cause they know that I can sting
So I can fly where 'ere I like and savour everything.

An open window's calling me, think I'll investigate.
Looks like someone's just finished tea – there's jam upon that plate!

I crawl up close and lick my lips and try the tasty treat.
No matter that there's folk nearby – I hear their heavy feet!

Suddenly a magazine is slammed upon the plate.
Now was that meant to clobber me? It's just a second late!

Oh what a shame they're taking all the dishes to be washed.
I'll take the hint – I'm outa here – it's not my day to be squashed!

Flight of Fancy

I woke up one morning to find I'd grown wings.
Yes. Can you believe it? One out of each shoulder!
Well, I jumped off the bed, but it wasn't high enough,
So, I found something tall and gradually got bolder.

I started off gently so's not to scare folk,
But the look on their faces was great to behold.
Oh, the freedom I felt as I went further afield
And with lightness of body, I no longer felt old.

Some people looked up with their mouths all agape,
So, I laughed and called out "No, you're not in a dream".
I tried not to look in folk's bedroom windows
As I flew off to explore a field and a stream.

Over the cows and on to the woods,
Startling the birds that were roosting on high.
Some took off and joined me – curious, not scared,
And I laughed and I sang as they looked me in the eye.

Then higher I went, but something felt wrong,
My wings had lost strength and I plunged with a croak.
The ground came to meet me – frighteningly fast
But just at that moment – from my dream I awoke!

In the Grip of the Invisible Monster

I'm just about to drop off when I'm grabbed around the calf
And if you'd have seen me hit the floor, you'd have had a real good laugh.
I normally do a log roll to get out of my bed
But when cramp hits, I just don't think, it goes right out my head.

My blood pressure drops and I wobble like an egg
But all I can think of is the pain in my leg.
So, I stretch it and walk, holding on to the wall
Until it subsides, then back to bed I crawl.

Another time my toe does a cross-over thing
And like a girl possessed, out of bed I do spring.
Why is it so painful, this tiny little toe?
And why does the monster take so long to let go?

Now cramp in the thigh is the worst you can get.
It can make you swear and can make you sweat.
I'm touching my toes to stretch the damn thing
And contorting my body 'til my ears start to ring.

So why do my muscles keep giving me cramp
And tighten so much like I'm in a clamp?
Who can tell me how I can win the fight
With the invisible monster who grabs in the night?

The Age Gap Rap

I'm just an older lady on a walkie to my town
But there's other older strollers who can really get me down.
Get outa my way!

We have to queue so patiently in every single shop.
My back is aching crazy, man, I think I'm gonna drop.
Get outa my queue!

The younger generation have their eyes glued on their phones,
They don't see me approaching 'cause I'm just a bag of bones.
Get outa my face!

I thought about a buggy so I can run 'em down,
Or get a shopping trolley but I haven't got a pound.
Get outa my space!

I've been and done my shopping and I'm dropping to my knees,
I've gotta find a bit of oomph before I start to wheeze.
I'm outa this place!

The Sticky End

One day we will surely peg out
And whether we're Baptist or Quaker
We'll all have to kick the bucket
And go and meet our Maker.

Yes, some will snuff it quickly,
Some gradually pass away,
But however we bite the dust
We'll all return to clay.

Some may give up the ghost
'Cause this world is full of strife.
Some may not want to perish
But we all depart this life.

Many deny it will happen,
Think their life will never expire.
We could try and stay safe indoors
Or be bold and play with fire.

You may not care how you go,
Say "Once I'm gone, I'm gone."
But I'll just say "Make sure
You've got clean underwear on!"

The Lost Stripes

One day, in the jungle, a young tiger looked up and, just overhead,
Just within reach perhaps, he saw a dark shape which was humming.
Tigger could smell the sweet honey and wondered what it would taste like,
So – up he reached with extended claws – and grabbed!
Oh dear, honey dribbled down his limbs and covered his body.
The angry bees buzzed around him and off he ran and ran.
Coming to some sand, he rolled around
Until he had rid himself of the stinging swarm.
Next was to rinse all the sticky goo from his beautiful body, but –
As he looked at his reflection in the pool he got a shock!
What was this pale yellowy creature that was looking back at him?
Frightened, the young tiger backed off. He didn't know what had happened.
He decided to look down into the pool from the safety of a nearby rock –
Yes, that strange yellow creature was still there.
Unfortunately, his sticky feet slipped from under him
And down he splashed, right on to the sandy creature in the pool.
He fought that unknown monster with thrashing arms and legs
And bared teeth, but couldn't quite catch it
Until, exhausted, he hauled himself out and sat panting on the edge.
As the monster hadn't got him, he felt brave enough now to have another look,
But, only his reflection was there,
With his beautiful stripes glowing on his dark gold body.
Phew, that was a close shave!

Space Bake

I was lucky enough to join the crew
Of the International Space Station,
So I packed my bags with all the things
You'd take for a long vacation.

But, instead of books, crosswords and cozzie
I took ingredients and baking trays.
Officials tutted and raised eyebrows,
Others said "It's just a phase".

So, up in space we all unpacked
And I got funny looks
As out came packets, mixer and scales
And a couple of thick cook books.

Day one I did experiments
With scientific stuff,
But I was dying to bake a cake
Or a tart or nice cream puff.

Day two I got ingredients out
But, oh what a shock I got,
When the flour became a foggy cloud
And the egg wouldn't stay in the pot.

There was an awful mess in the cabin that day,
All covered with sticky white dust,
But after 50 minutes of heat
We all sported the perfect pie crust!

My One Hour Dilemma

My Internet bundle allows me just
One hour to make my call.
Over that and I have to pay
So, I'm up against the wall.

The answerphone tells me that I am now
Number sixteen in the queue
So, I tap my feet as the music plays
Then go and make a brew.

Half an hour later I'm number eight,
The service is quite shoddy.
A voice keeps telling me it's quicker on line
But I want to speak to a body.

I start to fret as I wonder if
I'll understand their accent,
And suddenly trying on line appears
To have a certain attraction.

We're up to fifty-five minutes now
And I'm still only number four.
"That's it" I shout as I slam it down,
"I can't wait anymore!"

Shedding Ideas

I've the bud of an idea for a poem, it concerns some sort of tree.
In my mind the green shoots are showing, will I twig it?
I'll try it and see.

Now I'm quaking like an aspen, I can't see the wood for the trees.
I'm in the autumn of life and I may fall on my knees.

Should it be gnarled and twisted, a winter skeleton, bare?
Or fully dressed for summer with juicy fruit everywhere?

Has it knowledge of good and evil in the Garden of Eden today?
If I eat the fruit of temptation, will there be hell to pay?

No – momentum is sapped, my fervent hope is stemmed,
I can't branch out more than the poem I've just penned!

Pandemic Prose 2020 to Whenever

What a shock to the nation when the virus arrives –
after all it's not hives.
It's a killer, this thing, it's sneaky, invisible, horrible, miserable.
The government hasn't a clue.
Grey suits don't know what to do.
Their plans all go wrong, where's that PPI?
Pie in the sky 'til the people muck in,
Making masks in their dining rooms and scrubs in their lounges.
Lock up the town! Shut all shops down!
No schools or pubs, no cafes or crowds.
Zap this virus where it hurts,
But some people ignore and it comes back for more.
Economy bad – so sad. Let's do a cheap meal deal so the restaurants heal.
Summertime, we're feeling fine, joy in our hearts, so sublime.
Schools and unis open again, bringing more death and pain.
It's lurking round the corner. Don't you know it? It won't show it.
Boom! It mutates rather quick, there's so many sick.
Hospitals full again, death toll shocking so –
Lockdown number 2, but what good will it do?
We're open again, too soon, so the Christmas shops can gain
And some people can visit their loved ones.
They spread their love and they spread the bug.
So, come January, Lockdown number 3,
but vaccine's on the scene, which means, hope's on the horizon.

One year to the day – it hasn't gone away.
It's not under control but it's getting that way.
We're looking at Spring – what joy it will bring.
Can't wait to garden and go out walking –
Meet up with friends, do lots of talking.
Our second summer comes and goes.
The daily graph still has highs and lows.
But we seem to be getting used to it –
Bad idea or just life?
Travelling, shopping, all our daily tasks,
Mostly without masks.
The government's u-turns are a thing to behold –
Wonder if this will last as long
As the Spanish Flu, a hundred years ago.

Lockdown Town

The precinct's normally vibrant with us locals out a'shoppin'
And teenagers just standing round with nothing much to do.
There's normally folk from out of town and tourists for the day
Waiting for the next train home or looking for a loo.

I usually have to be aware of boys on speeding bikes
Or kiddies running, having fun, escaping Dad or Mum.
The pubs and cafés are usually full of happy hungry folk.
There's music, chatter, laughing and I don't think anyone's glum.

But on my walk the other day it's not like this at all!
The shops have got their shutters down and there's no lights inside.
The precinct's almost empty and the cafs are dark and bleak.
I felt depressed and lonely, and many a time I sighed.

Then all at once the lockdown eased, masked people walk about.
The atmosphere has changed and I'm happy that's for sure,
Optimism's in the air, good times are on their way.
We feel the heady freedom and the precinct smiles once more.

Speeding Along the Prom

Oh, what fun when you're old and grey
To be out along the prom,
But I can't walk as far as the beach
Now my muscles have up and gone.

So, for those places, a scooter I bought,
(The ones you sit on, I mean)
Now, with a friend, we decide where to scoot
And we leave, keen to go full-steam.

Well, we jolt and we bump 'cause the pavement's not flat
But other people share our space
And my hooter makes such a pitiful noise
That I just go slow with good grace.

Now, at certain times, the prom is quite bare.
We decide to up the pace,
So, with joy in our hearts and wind in our hair
We do a four-miles-an-hour race.

Well, it's a challenge to get ahead
But my rival's made a mistake.
'Cause she got too close as I decided to stop
She forgot, scooters don't have a brake!

The Twelve Weeks to Christmas

Christmas is a-coming and I'm making lots of plans,
The sort that come in bottles and the sort that come in cans.
Now shall I buy a gateau or shall I make a flan?
Still – twelve weeks to go!

Where is all the tinsel and the candles from last year?
I've got to get it all just right to make an atmosphere.
The tree is looking tatty but a new one's much too dear.
Still – 11 weeks to go!

So, shall we invite relatives or just friends for the day?
And if they have too much to drink, will they want to stay?
Or shall we risk eternal wrath – just pack and go away?
Just 10 weeks to go!

What shall we buy old Auntie Maud and twenty cousins – plus?
What did we get them last year? And what did they give us?
If we didn't get them anything, would they kick up a fuss?
Just 9 weeks to go!

Someone's sent an early card – I haven't bought mine yet!
The shops are putting pressure on, I've just begun to fret.
If I give in to everything I'm going into debt!
Aaagghh, just 8 weeks to go!

The shops ring out their Christmas songs 'bout Santa and his sleigh.
There's lots of sparkly glitter and pretend snow on display.
I take a very big deep breath and dive into the fray.
Aaagghh, just 7 weeks to go!

So I'm buying food and presents and more tinsel for the tree.
I've mixed the pud and made the cake and mince pies for thirty-three.
I haven't got time for anything else, not friends or family.
Aaagghh, just 6 weeks to go.

But then I think – what am I like? What's all this worry for?
Some people have got no-one – some people are dirt poor.
Some people can't buy presents and some sleep on the floor.
Mmmm and still 5 weeks to go.

We all have different sorts of lives, yet we all celebrate
The birth of Jesus, sent to earth, God's love to demonstrate.
But do we know him in the midst of unfairness and hate?
Mmmm only 4 weeks to go.

Lots of prophets wrote about the Saviour of Mankind,
How he would come in humility and open the eyes of the blind,
And how he's like a treasure we should all seek to find.
Mmmm 3 weeks to go.

Wow, what a loving God we have – he wants us all to know
How much he cares for each of us – sent Jesus here to show
That we can know God personally, and see the way to go.
Mmmm 2 weeks to go.

Well now I know what Christmas is really all about
I've got a smile upon my face – my worries I kicked out
And with all other revellers I can really sing and shout.
Wey hey – only 1 week to go!

We've done as much as we can do and all have played their part.
The morning's dawned, it's Christmas Day, such joy should fill our hearts.
We finally got priorities right – let the celebrations start!
It's here at last – Happy Christmas!

Reigning for Seventy Years

Several generations have only known one monarch
Which doesn't happen often as you know,
So we are very blessed to have Elizabeth as Queen,
A stable head of state in highs and lows.

With Philip by her side through almost all her rule
And with her on most stately trips abroad,
She's done most everything that's asked of her
And kept her loyal people reassured.

The golden coach and sparkling crown of Coronation fame
Were seen by millions on a new TV.
Then Silver, Gold and Diamond celebrations
Now it's a Platinum Jubilee!

We saw her castle burning and divorces of her kids
At her 'annus horribilis' we were sad
But now we watch as great grandchildren
Light up her face and make her glad.

So, however many flags are waved at parties in our streets,
And, however many times we shout "Three cheers!"
You have to admit she's done well to reign
For seventy glorious years.

Other Publication by this Author

Oasis Moments
Poems, Prose & Songs for Inspiration and Encouragement